THE 4 TEAMS

THAT MAKE OR BREAK YOUR BUSINESS,
AND YOU

KERRY WOOD

Life is not a dress rehearsal

Book Layout © Million-Dollar-Author 2021

The 4 teams. That make or break your business… And you -- 1st edition.

ISBN: 978-0-6450942-3-7

What people have to say about 4 teams and working with Kerry Wood

Kerry assisted in defining our company values and involved the team in integrating them through behaviours into our operation. These activities and the visibility of the commitment from all has dramatically changed and improved our retention of staff and positively impacted our absenteeism. One of the side benefits of this has been that in the recruitment area our team members now bring their relations and friends when we have vacancies.

A.G. Manufacturing

Kerry brings an incredibly unique and direct approach working with us in our business. His approach is transparent, honest, and very driven, assisting us to achieve our business goals.

CH Import and Distribution Company

We have been working with Kerry for three years. He is an important part of our team and our company culture, and fun factor has changed dramatically over that time. The net effect has been to lift the efficiency and profitability through both the manufacture and installation areas of our business.

RL Construction Company

Kerry brings a wide range of business skills and knowledge to the table. His ability to cut through the dross and offer insightful and honest assessment of the situation has been a major contributor to our business success.

AH Mechanical Engineering

Attending Kerry's workshops has really assisted me to drive my business forward. The ability to plan and see the future clearly has been extremely helpful in making our business decisions.

AF Electrical Construction

Kerry listens intently and involves himself in every part of our business. He brings a real-world knowledge to business challenges and offers solutions that are easy to understand and put in place. His strategic and tactical knowledge appears endless, and our business has benefited greatly by having him on board.

LM Professional Services.

Acknowledgements

To the Family who support me through all.

My three kids: Chaos, Mayhem and Trouble (Alexander, Daniel and Sophie). Thanks for the space, time, fun and never a dull moment.

To Lee (my wife), always working for my best outcome and making us the best we can be.

About the Author

Businessman, father, champion musician, motor sport representative…. and author.

Kerry is a previous New Zealand and Australian Champion musician, NZ Representative power boat driver, Fight For Life boxing champion, Italian gourmet sous chef, regional hockey player, multiple-company CEO, national marketing executive, franchise owner, International Musical Director, graduate of the University of Technology in Marketing Management, and holds an LTCL performance diploma from the Royal Schools of Music.

Kerry believes that life is not a dress rehearsal, and that if you are going to do it then you must put 110% into it. Whether the activity is business, music or sport Kerry believes that it is your attitude, intention and intensity that will bring you the success you desire and deserve.

Kerry has owned and sold businesses ranging from the construction industry through to Software development and distribution, along with several other aligned companies. But most of all, Kerry enjoys mentoring, coaching and helping others to find their sweet spot.

CONTENTS

Chapter one

WHAT MAKES A GOOD TEAM?

A good man under stress....

Hamish was an amazing plumber, but when we caught up a couple of Christmases ago, he looked to me like the world was resting on his shoulders. Really deep pain in the eyes and just the slumped shoulders that showed he was carrying a lot of big stuff around.

He looked that average, that I put my hand on his shoulder and said, "*Are you OK mate*?" He looked me in the eye, that look that says you never told me - why didn't you warn me - and said quite directly "*you have no idea the hell pit that I'm living in.* "

I looked him straight back in the eye and said, "*I'll get the coffee and let's hear the tale of woe*", all the time thinking it was teenagers - or maybe he couldn't get enough work for his business.

I first met Hamish a few years ago at a music event, and I well remember the skip in his step, and the light in the eyes as we shared stories about how well we played that day in Christchurch.

He was equally excited because he just set up his business. To hear him talk then, well the world was not ready for the adventure and excitement he was bringing to the game.

But now he started, *"Do you have any idea how hard it is to engage your staff, so they actually care? How on earth am I meant to manage my business when I can only rely on myself to be 100% reliable? The bottom line is, all my customers are only interested in price, and my suppliers don't give a damn.*

Worse still, every now and again when I go home, I just want an inch of quiet. Ten minutes to think about how I deal with what I have to deal with."
And then he finished with *"They reckon no man's an island - well some bugger has marooned me here!!"*

Hamish is not alone; many business owners experience the desire to master the soul-sucking quest to make things better in their business.

If you are like most people, you're reading this book looking for ideas to sort out what you see as your team or staff members' failure to meet your expectations.

You may see your team as not engaged, not motivated, not reliable, not committed.

Your business would be so much more profitable if you as the business owner were working on your own - only had yourself to worry about, to work with and get the job done!

One of the things I often hear is:
I wish I had 3, 6, 25 people who worked as hard, were as committed and reliable as I am!

Your stress around working with your team members, recruiting good people, constantly managing problems, training staff and the apparent lack of reward they feel, can really weigh on you.

However, if you develop your four teams - yes four! - into four high-performing units, then profit improves, stress disappears, and you get your enjoyment of the business back.

In the last ten years of business coaching, consulting, and thirty years of being in business, the constant themes that come back to me from business owners about their teams are the same.

There can be a massive disconnect between what the owner communicates, needs, and desires and what the team or staff member expects, can deliver and wants to do. And then there are the outcomes that are required by the organisation to be successful.

To say this is a communication gap is an understatement. Part is communication, part is expectation, part is the ability to see the big picture, and part is an inability to listen to the other person's point of view.

No one person or organisation is at fault here, it is just the way of it. Business owners and business managers will say it is "*the way of the world*", "*the way of the new generation*", or a new time, and it is impossible to get good staff.

And this is before we even start considering the fact of how these people are paid, what their position descriptions might be or what their reasonable future prospects are with the company. I'm frequently reminded of the old proverb that *"you get what you expect"*, or the other saying *"life is a mirror"*. Mmmmmm…..

So how do you sit down with the business owner and start working on the teams that they think will make their life easier, their business more successful, and in fact make them more profit?

The realisation of these commonalities in just about every business, through every business segment, through every business size, has led me to question the outcomes that the business manager or owner actually wants.

Because we must agree that the reason for doing anything is for an outcome - to have staff or a team around you, you must want an outcome?

So, the obvious start point is: what outcome do you want?

The outcomes would seem to be quite simple. That is, we want more **consistent**, more **engaged** and more **reliable** team members. And if we had these then all our problems would be solved!

It is far too easy for the business owner to place the blame fair and square on the team or the staff. Often, the behaviour or performance of the team is a very direct reflection of the business owner.

While the business owner may see themselves as reliable, consistent, and engaged, these are the three qualities or three descriptions that everybody sees differently. So, the most important thing is that we have an agreement as to what they all mean.

Effectively we need to build frameworks around behaviour, because there is an old business saying: "*without a framework it will be hard work or guesswork"*. The better the framework, the better the result.

Reliability as a personal trait is something that as a team leader, business owner or manager, you need to expect and **inspect**. The social proof or a lack of reliability is easy to find. Such things as arriving late to work, not completing a task in time for the deadline, not turning up in the right uniform - these are very visible and obvious signs of a lack of reliability.

Less obvious evidence of a lack of reliability is such things as failure to upsell in a sales environment, not greeting your clients well in a retail environment, and not making sure that the task assigned to you is done in the best way possible. Reliability is a key asset in any team or staff member, and has to be taught, encouraged, recognised, respected, loved and applauded.

If the desire is **Engagement**, the reality is disengagement. This shows itself in many ways.

The first is a lack of interest in the performance of the company, or the performance of the job, or the performance of a task.

Lack of engagement is further evidenced by the inability and/or lack of desire to communicate well, politely, respectfully - well let's use the word humorously - with clients to create a great client experience. This disengagement also shows itself as a lack of referral for the work that you as a company do.

Part of disengagement would also be demonstrated by a higher turnover of staff and probably less interaction at team meetings, health and safety meetings, and product development meetings.

Disengagement is the hardest thing to measure, but the most apparent in a business or team. In his book *Good to Great*, Jim Collins talks about *"getting the right people on the bus"*. This is exactly what Engagement does - it brings the right people onto the bus at the right time to do the right task.

Further evidence of disengagement can be seen when a team member "decides" to leave the office or the workshop just before the job is finished - just before the actual task is complete. Because to them completing the task or completing the job means nothing. Sound familiar?

"Decides" means nothing – it is a version of "they don't care". This is a simple way of saying disengaged. Often business owners make the mistake of thinking that money, or some style of reward will change disengagement. This is exactly the wrong thing to do as disengagement comes from a raft of thoughts, emotions, and behaviours. As we will see later in the book, being **Engaged** is about involvement, review, respect, and success.

So, if **Reliability** is doing what we are there to do, and doing it well, respectfully and on time; and **Engagement** is doing it with love and making the company or the team that you work for the focus of what you're doing at that time; then **Consistency** is a methodology, measurement and visibility where both of these are tied together to deliver the same outcome over and over and over again.

Anybody can deliver a great performance once. There is a musical saying that *"perfect practice makes perfect performance"*. And it has never been truer than it is in business.

So as a business owner or leader you must set expectations, train those expectations, then manage and report those expectations. Then the most important thing is to reward, respect and encourage those performance-based behaviours. This is **Consistency**.

As I mentioned before, you and your business have **four teams.**

And you as a leader, manager and business owner have to develop, drive, embrace and model the three behaviours of Engagement, Reliability and Consistency across ALL of your four teams!

Yes – FOUR teams! And you have to instill the values, the behaviours, and leadership across the four teams to make sure that you get rid of the stress and get the benefits that you as a business owner deserve.

The bottom line is that in years of working with business owners, I have found that business owners, managers and leaders tend to get the teams or constituents they deserve. If there is a clear set of guidelines - an agreed set of values and outcomes - then the teams will function well.

That is not to say there won't be discussion or even disagreement. But we are all on a journey together, and the four teams all helix or connect to provide you the business owner, you the manager, you the leader with a less stressful, more successful, and less time-demanding role.

In the following chapters we will discover and define the four teams. I will show you how to get the best behaviours out of your teams, and how to lead the teams in a simple but effective way.

We will spend time on Direction. There are more books written on leadership than on cooking! So, let's take action and create direction! You have to direct and lead your teams. You must have a communication style that is uniquely yours, and a set of values that are displayed, reasonable and agreed.

Your business is a mirror. The best and worst of your business is reflection of the best and worst in you

We will discuss and agree on the Rules of the Game, how we bring new players onto our teams, and how to develop our audition and recruitment strategies. Then we will have a look at the tools you need. In this book, you will find Action Plans, Worksheets and Matrix tools designed to be easy-to-use tools that you can use to make a difference. None of the tools in this book are complex – they are all approachable and effective.

Directing a team and building a group of people to achieve great things, is one of the most rewarding parts of life. It's not only about the camaraderie and success, but it's about seeing people grow and develop in front of you. It's about looking at their families and how they benefit from your business, from your leadership. It's about the impact you can have on the community, the industry, your family and everyone around you. Because you have a great set of four teams, and it is your leadership that will get them humming.

Chapter Two

YOUR 4 TEAMS

How tough are you? How hard are you? How many challenges can you overcome, and can you do it all on your own?

When I was called in by the wife of a business owner recently, the tone in her voice told me something was wrong. Very wrong.

The business was rocking along OK, but her husband's health - I mean his head health, his mental health - had collapsed. This was having a physical effect as well. The stress, the worry, the constant stuff that goes on when you employ a team had finally taken its toll.

In a conversation he reiterated many of the themes I have heard in my years of business coaching:

"I just have to do it all. Even when I pay them more than they're worth, they don't turn up. I've had a consultant and we have all the bonus schemes, but they still don't do a constant job."

I listened and talked some more and found out a little bit about the stress, the time, the bank - but also the fun as well, and how the business was going. The business was profitable. The business was trading well. The business had a great brand; had a great digital footprint. Overall, it was on the up and up!

Sitting in the room his partner was aghast at the stress. It was not that she didn't have a clue. It was that she did not realise how deep and wide the river was. We had a brief discussion about his clients; how loyal they were and how we could rely on them. He assured me they were all great clients, provided he gave him the best price. Some had been with him for a long time, but other than that he knew little about them.

We spoke about his suppliers and in short, he had little to say that was good about them.

Then I asked a very simple question:
"*Who, in your support network do you celebrate with? You know, when you win a deal, have a great month or year. Who could we have a conversation with to provide you with some support; some conversation?*"

He thought about it for a minute and then said:

"This is my business; I make the decisions. I don't tell many people about what's going on - including the wife!"

The stress around working with team members, recruitment, the constant management and training and the apparent lack of reward really weighs on the owner. They feel very alone in it.

I pursued the question: "*Who do you celebrate with? When you do a great job when you've had a great month do you take the wife out for dinner? If it's been a great quarter do you take the family away for the weekend?*"

For the first time he laughed heartily and said yes, he and his wife had a couple of favourite restaurants that they went out to when things were great. No, they didn't do a weekend thing with the family. That he had a boat, took his boys fishing, and then he asked me if I had any idea how much petrol cost when you were water skiing with three teenage boys!

Who do you celebrate with? And how do you celebrate?

So, then I asked the question slightly differently and said: "*Tell me how you celebrate with your team at work?* " He looked me in the eye and told me that if the guys had been working well then, he sometimes brought a few pizzas and maybe put on a couple of drinks. But nothing structured.

So, no structure. NO!

I then asked him the big question:

"*So, do you think your work team, and your suppliers are informed enough, know what's successful for you, and give you good feedback on how well they are tracking and how well things are going?*"

NO! His silence said it all.

"*You know that all human beings really want to be successful, don't you? You know that the people who work for you, and the people who work with you, and the people who are around you all want to be successful, don't you? Successful in their own way in their own world? So, you need to give them the road map, the pathway to be successful in their world.*"

He cheered up. "*So you're talking about telling them where we're at, and how we want to succeed?*"

"*Eureka*" said I – "*you got it!*"

So, the news is all good: you actually have FOUR teams and seriously they all want you to succeed and have more time, have more fun, be less stressed and make more money!

Just use the simple stuff following in this book, and you will develop your four business teams (yes 4!!) into four high-performing units. Profit improves, stress disappears, and you get your enjoyment of the business back.

Let's define the 4 Teams and show you how this will really help you as a business owner or manager.

In defining the four teams that make or break your business and you, we're actually defining the whole ecosystem that supports you as a successful business owner.

This ecosystem provides you with support, knowledge, and motivation to be the best business owner and leader you can be and have the best business that you can have.

The four teams in your business are:

1	The Staff	Think about:
	The staff, the employees, the band members, the players, etc.	Those who do the stuff
2	The Clients	
	Clients, Audience, Prospects, Supporters, the Database, etc.	Those who get the outcome of what you do, those whose problems you solve
3	The Suppliers	
	Suppliers, Venues, Providers, the Authorities, the Clubs, the Associations	Those who rely on you for their success, and you use to create outcomes for Team 2
4	Home	
	Family, Friend, Partners, Mentors, Ourselves	Those there at the beginning and end. Who benefit or see your success and share in your joy and stress

Team 1 – Your Staff

These are the people who do the stuff that you want them to do. The people who make you money. These are the people that you lead all the time.

Team 2 – Your Clients

Your clients are the people who pay you. These are the people who are receiving the outcomes of your business or service.

Team 3 – Your Suppliers

These are the people who provide you with stuff to allow you to do the services or sell the things you do. Nearly every business owner I deal with does not realise they can influence them, and the light that they can and should be.

Team 4 – Your Home Support

Your home support team. The way to think about this is the people that you celebrate with when something goes well in the business. The people who benefit when you can afford a new car. The people who you buy a drink for. The individuals that you've known awhile, that know you - that possibly have seen you succeed (or not succeed) before. You decide the parameters here.

These four teams create the ecosystem of your business.

The same values that you put into your life and put into your business, you also put into your teams. If one team is not acting in harmony with the other teams, the whole ecosystem collapses.

In the next chapter we will introduce you to a measuring system: the *Team Drive Quotient* matrix. This will allow you to look at your four teams and know where you can improve - where you can already lead well, and where you should do more work.

Every business I've worked with that has focus on all four teams does well. The business has a great relationship with its suppliers who support everything they do. They have a great relationship with their clients who aren't so price-focused that it causes the business challenges.

Developing your home support network with the same passion, thought and process as you develop your business team, clients and suppliers, gives the business owner a tremendous amount of support, fun and more success.

It makes celebrating the wins so much more enjoyable when everybody knows what's going on. And it makes the loneliness that can happen when things get a little bit tough so much easier to bear. Because people around you can support you and know what's going on (you decide *how much* they know!)

The four teams that make or break you and your business are not a fad. It's not a rumor or some academic thought pattern. It's the real world!

You have all these teams around you. You have all of these resources available to you.

To be a successful business owner you need to grab hold of these and really make them work. Read on - you'll love it!

THE FOUR TEAMS

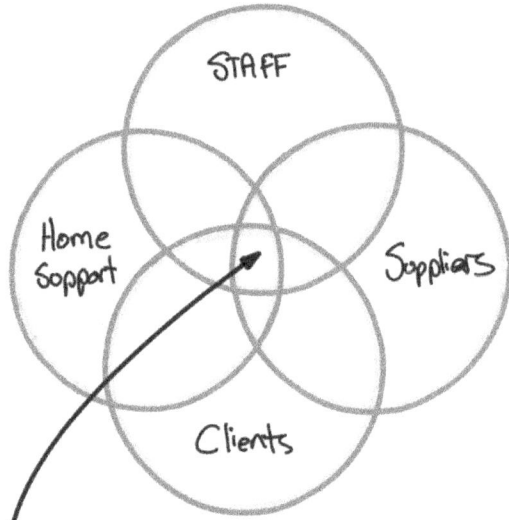

STAFF

Home
Support

Suppliers

Clients

Live in the
Sweet Spot

Chapter Three

WHAT YOU WANT AND WHAT YOU GET

The Myth. The Reality. The Teams we get!

You have just read that in any business you have four teams. So now you're probably a wee bit scared!

You are probably thinking: I was exhausted when I thought I had just one team. Now you are telling me I've got four?!

But this does not mean four times the work. In fact, it should mean do something well once, and just enjoy running it into the other teams

So, first of all, let's define what we want out of our teams and what we usually end up getting.

Our four teams, let's recap what they are:

1. **Our Business team** – our participants, our players of the game
2. **Our Clients** – our prospects, our audience, our supporters
3. **Our Suppliers** – our venues, our providers
4. **Our Home team** – our partners, our friends, our mentors, ourselves.

It's really interesting that when we look to build our teams across all four areas, we are looking for the same things. The same values and really the same performance.

The four teams we desire and the four teams we end up with, are usually from what is sometimes described as a "parallel universe"! That is - looking similar but not even close to what we thought we wanted!

When we recruit to get the kind of teams we want around us, we are looking for three things:

- We're looking for **Consistency**
- We're looking for **Reliability**
- We're looking for **Engagement**.

Let us start with **Engagement**.

Engagement is that thing in a team member that shows they care. That shows they want the best for the business, the client, the supplier, and the owner or the manager, you.

Engagement is about how they might recommend your business or your operation to other people, both from a client point of view and a new team member point of view. There is no better team member than one that is recommended to you. Engagement comes from always trying to develop the best knowledge for your business, for your client, for the exact situation.

This is the same across ALL FOUR TEAMS!
Looking into the office and seeing someone just finishing a report at ten minutes past finishing time is Engagement. That is, the desire to finish the job to get it done, so that they deliver what you expect and get satisfaction from it. Engagement.

Engagement goes hand in hand with knowledge and learning. If you are engaged in what you're doing, then you will want to develop yourself, to learn. The development is not only learning and looking beyond where we are at, but it's also innovation. That is, looking to constantly improve and develop what we are doing for the betterment of the person, the business, and the client.

It's also learning from experience. If we've done this one way and it works, let's take a little bit of a risk and try it another way - it could end up more effective. But always be engaged in the best outcome for the person, the client, or the business. Core evidence of Engagement is development. That is the ability to innovate, to learn and to gain from this experience. It drives the team and the individual forward to gain knowledge through questioning and having a worldly appreciation of what would be the best outcome for the team, the business, and the organization. This is about engagement in the future.

Part of the Engagement criteria sits with the ability to listen and be focused on what is the best outcome for the business, and the best outcome for the customer.

Engagement is that quality in a team member when you know that they have your back. That they are behaving in the best way for the business.

Think it through - **all four** of your teams have to be Engaged.

Reliability is a symptom or a visual cue of Engagement.

Reliability is one of the most important attributes you can look for in a team member or a staff member. It's pointless having the best brain surgeon in the world if they don't turn up to do the operation!

One of the basics of Reliability is timeliness. That is not only turning up on time or in time to start work but working in a manner that is reliable and expected from you and your client or suppliers. Reliability goes to the quality that is being turned out, and at the same time being able to deliver KPIs to a quality level that you would expect.

One of the cues of Reliability is respect. If you have someone that's engaged and reliable, then they are respectful of the business environment, the team environment and the client environment. Reliability, respect, and timeliness bring out the attribute of thoughtfulness. This aligns to the quality of delivering a quality outcome all the time. You can base your business on a reliable team member. This will be indicated by key performance indicators and results in the future.

Consistency is what this all adds up to. Consistency in delivery. Consistency in attitude. Consistency and respect. Consistency in every area of the business.

One of the core areas of Consistency is the area of skills or knowledge. When you have qualifications or skills that are provable, socially provable, academically provable, and provable by performance, then consistently this will benefit the team and the team member.

A key component of a consistent team member, consistent staff member or consistent support person is will. The will to be the best they can be. The will to be what they can before you. The will to be the support person and the open, honest person you wish to be involved with. This will come down to being future based. We all desire to be successful and a successful team. Successful team members and a successful director or leader is always future based.

Again, think it through - all four of your teams have to be **Consistent**.

In a consistent mind set, communication is paramount. Whether the communication is feedback which is delivered in a positive, reliable, respectful and timely fashion. Or whether it's delivered in a short meeting or a huddle.

Communication through technology and reporting is also imperative to consistency.

Big goals start with small steps

Small steps taken every day will be a major leap forward in every business – just like in every sport. There are many sayings about taking small steps to achieve major goals and consistency is about exactly that. My favorite is:

"Big goals start with small steps."

Consistent small steps. Consistent leadership. Consistent direction will get us the big goals.

Every human being wants to be successful. So, by having consistent small steps and by having consistent, reliable and engaged teams we will achieve what you want to achieve.

Consistency is putting the small Lego or building blocks in place to build your business that you then know is going to happen.

Consistency, **Reliability** and **Engagement**. These three words are the basis of every person who tries to put a team together. But while we may start with these great outcomes in mind, what we usually end up with is exactly (or close to) the opposite!

There are many very visual and behavioural things that you can see in what I would call a dysfunctional team. A team that is delivering nearly the opposite of what we wanted when we first started to build a team around us.

The first demonstration is usually an uncommunicative approach - what you may see as even deceitful or dishonest.

Teams that are not engaged and teams that are not lead/directed in a consistent fashion can become very reward focused. This leads to short-term, and at times exceptionally transient, changes. The reward-driven approach means that they are not focused on the outcome for the team, or for the company.

This is a four-team dilemma.

You will recognise some of the symptoms of an average team: missing deadlines, watching the clock, making a very quick exit right on finish time without finishing a job that has to be done.

Bad or badly lead/directed teams who are not consistent or respectful will not only be demanding of your time, but also demanding of rewards, and recognition for everything they do.

The old adage "the squeaky wheel gets the most oil" is a common saying for teams that have stopped being reliable, consistent and engaged.

Teams that are not consistent, engaged and reliable will have an awful lot of noise around what they're actually doing and what they are achieving - not where they're going or what they need to achieve. This is in the hope of getting more and more rewards, and more and more of your time.

One of the key visual or behavioural cues of a team that is not consistent, that is not reliable and that is not displaying engaged personality traits, is a sporadic performance.

That is being unpredictable.

At times they will really perform well. You will look at this and say: "I've got a great team!" But this will be very sporadic. There will be lows where they will not be consistent. There will be deadlines missed, and there will be mistakes. And you will be looking at these and constantly fixing them.

Sometimes, there are even issues with honesty around quality. The misleading of delivering reports to make sure that you as the leader or the director see that they're doing well, when in fact they're hiding behind doing the minimum.

This self-serving nature means that at times the carelessness or just the failure to detail will mean they are not consistent in their performance.

The most apparent function or obvious behaviour of a team that is not consistent, reliable, or engaged is a word I would use - selfish.

There is no community. What they do a little bit of is - I'm going to use the word dishonesty. Because they're not genuine in what they're trying to drive forward for the organisation or the business.

The selfishness comes down to the desire for reward and recognition for what they are doing. Again, this resonates with all four teams: Staff, Clients, Suppliers and Home.

So, what we want is a group of people, a team, an ensemble working together that is really really consistent. Consistent in the will and communication and really really engaged.

They are knowledgeable and learning, recommending of you, respectful and reliable. They demonstrate timeliness, meet deadlines and are really working with each other. They are harmonious.

That's what we want.

We can see and feel that the stress of having a team that is the opposite - sporadic, thoughtless, unreliable, and unpredictable. Demanding of your time, rewards and demanding of change and what I would call selfish. They are uncommunicative, and very inwardly reward focused. The stress as the leader here is huge.

All four teams:

- Our Business team - our participants, our players of our game
- Our Clients - our prospects, our audience, our supporters
- Our suppliers - our venues, our providers

- Our home team - our partners, our friend, our mentors, ourselves.

All four have the same needs, desires, emotions and require a similar (slightly nuanced) set of values, behaviours and thoughts to make them amazing.

Read on. We will put in place the road map and show you how to write the symphony to make this happen.

Chapter four

YOUR TEAM DRIVE QUOTIENT

The good news is…. there are some simple steps you can take to get your four teams working really well to support your business.

During this chapter I am going to introduce you to a tool called the **Team Drive Quotient.**

This is a set of numbers, a measure that you set up as a business owner or a manager to look at how your teams – yes, your four teams - are working. We will start with a single-team approach to your business.

Do the following little exercise.

Give yourself a mark out of 10 for the following things to show how your staff/Business team work with you - how your staff members are working:

- Do you acknowledge you have a team around you? (Score yourself /10)

- How well do you communicate with your team? (Again, score yourself /10)

- How well do you involve your team in decisions about what's going on in the business? (Again, score /10)

- How well do you think you lead your team? (Now come on be honest - mark yourself /10)

- And how well do you think your team is engaged with your business? (Score yourself /10).

Just remember that in Australia and New Zealand only 26% of employees are engaged with the business in which they are employed. So how do you rate?

Let's look at a bit of an example, to show you how this tool works.

I have made up some sample numbers and placed these scores in a little table below.

Let's say we gave ourselves a strong 9/10 for acknowledging the team, a 5/10 for communicating with them, a 2/10 for involving them (because really it's your business and you make the decisions!), a 3/10 for leading them (because if you were leading them better you probably wouldn't be reading this book!) And for how much they are engaged you gave them a solid 2/10.

That gives you a total combined score of 21 out of a possible 50. Actually, in Australasia that's probably not a bad score for someone running one team:

Out Of 10	Acknowledge	Communicate	Involve	Lead	Engage	TOTAL /50	
Staff	9	5	2	3	2	21	42%

You will find that the more you involve your team in the business - that is the decisions, the direction, the visions and what we're doing - the more you will be seen as a leader and these numbers will grow.

But more about that later.

So, imagine if you actually ran a metric for **all your four teams**. That is - your team at work, your clients, your suppliers and your home support.

The thing is, you probably acknowledge you've got clients and you probably communicate with your clients in some form of basic newsletter. And, you probably acknowledge you have suppliers because you talk to them and pay them. So, the metric might look something like this:

	Acknowledge	Communicate	Involve	Lead	Engage	TOTAL /50		
							50	
Staff	9	5	2	3	2	21	42%	
Clients	2	2	0	0	0	4	8%	
Suppliers	2	0	0	0	0	2	4%	
Home	0	0	0	0	0	0	0%	
Quotient SCORE	13	7	2	3	2	27	200	14%

The above metric is how I have found 90% of businesses I've begun working with in the last few years. Not a metric or measure of the success of the business, but definitely a measure of the team dynamic, and therefore, the impact on the owner in time, stress, choice and in the end profit.

What it shows is that you do acknowledge your clients and you do communicate with a newsletter, that maybe 22% open and 12% read.

You do acknowledge your suppliers because you probably pay them.

But with the home support team, it is at this point (and usually is) a poor team result. But how often do we all see a company going into liquidation and when we see the family on the television, or in other media it's obvious that they have no clue what's going on?

With very little work, following some success behaviours and setting up Rules of the Game for everybody you work alongside and everyone who works alongside you, can have a massive effect on the Team Drive Quotient Metric.

So, in a typical business with an overworked, stressed owner with little time to lead or upskill – by the way, you're reading this book and you are upskilling!! - by acknowledging your suppliers, communicating with them and knowing that your suppliers want to be engaged with you, can make a world of difference. It's simple because you make them money. You trade with them and they need you.

By also working with your home network a little bit, the following total metric can be achieved:

	Acknowledge	Communicate	Involve	Lead	Engage	TOTAL		
							50	
Staff	9	5	2	3	2	21	42%	
Clients	5	3	3	2	2	15	30%	
Suppliers	2	2	2	2	5	13	26%	
Home	5	1	1	1	5	13	26%	
Quotient SCORE	21	11	8	8	14	62	200	31%

The number 21, which is the Staff Team Drive Quotient metric for when you are just looking at one team; on their own have limited impact. But you can see that by simply adding effort, communication and acknowledgement to the four teams, the number easily moves to 62.

Effectively a doubling of your "Team".

Always think of this approach as **rocket boosters for your business**.

Now while numbers are very subjective and these are all your opinion of how you're doing with these four teams, we would all agree that the more people/the more teams/the more focus you have on your business drives, the better the whole team will do. And these numbers are just indicators so you can track any change that you create.

We would all agree that if your clients, your suppliers, your staff team and your home support network are working with you, for you, they all see your goals and visions. Then the opportunity to succeed must improve.

Think of this as rocket boosters for your business

Conversely at times of stress, at times of needing support, you have more informed people to call on.

So, let's take another step and think about how we would look - how this four-team metric would look - if we put some solid work into this approach.

As we will work through in the following chapters of the book, it is a step-by-step process, not unlike the building blocks that children use, to build the four teams into a veritable wall of information and support for you. And better still, resulting in more profit and a reduction in stress.

By adopting some simple steps and changing behaviours, we can drastically move the Team Drive Quotient (TDQ). Every move towards the magic 200 (total possible) effectively removes stress, recruitment issues, and time from the business owner's day and adds dollars to the bottom line.

So, let's add a bit of effort, skill and knowledge to the relationship, engagement and therefore, performance of the four teams:

	Acknowledge	Communicate	Involve	Lead	Engage	TOTAL		
Staff	9	7	5	6	6	33	66%	
Clients	5	5	5	4	6	25	50%	
Suppliers	4	4	4	3	5	20	40%	
Home	5	5	5	5	5	25	50%	
Team drive	23	21	19	18	22	103	200	52%

This is an improvement by a factor of 300% from our first table!

And this is only 50% of the potential of what can be achieved by focusing on this approach.

In the above metric you can see that we've actually taken a strong ownership of our client base by acknowledging communicating with them and involving them. We can do this by various means. We actually even lead them, which is great. And by leading them and involving them, they will become more engaged.

Our suppliers we are acknowledging and we're communicating with them - involving them in our business decisions. This suits them as well. You will see that by involving them, they too become a lot more engaged in your business.

And lastly our home support team. The group of people around us who we celebrate with and rely upon. You will see that simply by acknowledging them as part of your business network, communicating with them, and involving them, they become more engaged.

It is important with the family home team, your support team, that there are boundaries. Like all teams, such as the staff team at work, you have boundaries for what you share with them. The suppliers again - there are boundaries with every team and the same with your clients. Every team has boundaries and rules. We will discuss this later.

You, by these simple changes, become a leader because they look to you.

Simply working with your four teams and developing them together through communication and acknowledgement strategies, plus leading them, will result in better engagement.

More engagement from your four teams will mean that the running of your business will become easier. You will be able to rely on people. You will be able to know that people are committed and engaged in what you do.

This will give you more time, more freedom, more choice, more profit, and at the end of the day - more fun!

So how does the leadership of your four teams rate currently, and where would you like to be in 6 months? Yes – in one year?

NOW

	Acknowledge	Communicate	Involve	Lead	Engage	Total
Staff						/50
Clients						/50
Suppliers						/50
Home						/50
Team drive						**/200**

DESIRED in 6 Months

	Acknowledge	Communicate	Involve	Lead	Engage	Total
Staff						/50
Clients						/50
Suppliers						/50
Home						/50
Team drive						**/200**

DESIRED in 12 Months

	Acknowledge	Communicate	Involve	Lead	Engage	Total
Staff						/50
Clients						/50
Suppliers						/50
Home						/50
Team drive						**/200**

Chapter Five

THE 3 STEP CHANGE PROCESS. DESIRE, A PLAN AND RESISTANCE

The business of Music.

A little while ago, I was invited to be the guest Musical Director of a group entering a national competition.

The organisation, the committee, the community were very desirous of winning this national competition. But looking at, shall we say the resources in the room, it was reasonably apparent that to win was going to be a challenge.

So, we put in place a plan. We started with the end date; this was the final performance. We worked out exactly where the whole organisation and all the individuals had to be every week on the journey, working back to the date that we were sitting around the meeting table.

We designed a rehearsal schedule that really worked hard on the areas that we knew the adjudication panel would be looking at. We worked out a rehearsal schedule that was fun, had a few barbecues and was not too onerous on time, involved the families, but was intensely quality focused.

We then searched around and found three or four great musicians who were prepared to assist in tuition and mentoring sections and individuals in the group.

The resistance. On presenting this plan to the committee, I received an interesting response. I was told: *We are a community organization, and as such, a focus on winning is in direct loggerheads with our community objectives.*

I agreed totally with the idea that this was a community organisation. And then I showed the committee the focus on family, on social activity, and growth as a musical entity and as individuals that was a key part of the plan. Surely this is what a community organisation is about?

The committee realised the plan was going to enhance membership, engagement and grow their community involvement.

NOTE….. Yes we won!!!

Unless you've got the desire to change, don't even bother.

Unless you want or desire change, or the "inner you" really talks to you and says: *"we need to change this"*, then the effectiveness of trying to drive your four teams to get a better result and be more successful in the business will be very challenging.

The following four chapters set up the 3-step change method by which you can dramatically change the performance of your four teams.

Step 1 – Desire to change

The first step in the three-step process is to decide that "yes, you really do wish to change".

The desire to change is the most powerful motivator.

The desire to change is defined by two factors: your dissatisfaction of the current situation, of where you are, multiplied by the vision of what you think could be, where you want to be, or the end game.

Dissatisfaction * Vision = Desire for Change

The more dramatically, graphically or intensely you can define the dissatisfaction, and the more amazing, colorful, beautiful the vision, the stronger the desire to change will be.

Let's start with the bad or negative… so Dissatisfaction.

There are many indicators of dissatisfaction, but let's start with ten quick questions:

1. Are you tired of your team not turning up on time?
2. Are you tired of them not delivering the results you require?

3. Does the constant retraining of your team members who don't seem to listen frustrate you?

4. Does no one listen to what you say and the instructions you give?

5. Do you feel you are carrying the burden of performance on your shoulders?

6. Is there no one you can confide in to ask what I would call an "honest question" and look for that great feedback?

7. When things go wrong, is there no one to sit down with and work through what we're going to do?

8. Is the commitment to the end game within the team not apparent?

9. Is there an absolute lack of consistency in performance and communication in your teams?

10. Do you feel that your teams have a "*what's in it for me*" attitude, and are not engaged in the bigger picture?

You may have a dozen other symptoms of a non-reliable, not consistent and disengaged team. So, come on - really define the dissatisfaction you have with this. If you answer one or two from the ten questions above, then you're probably not dissatisfied. If you answer more than four, then you probably are dissatisfied. If you answer 7 or 8 then you're heading towards really dissatisfied.

OK now the great stuff. The dream. The green fields. The blue-sky; the stuff you sing about in the shower!

The vision, the utopia. The "what-if" and "only I could dream about this".

So have a go now at thinking of what you would like to have happening in your team:

Your team turns up on time, dressed to work, and the first thing they say with a bit of humour and great attitude is "*good morning*!"

The attitude to "the brand" is great. In fact, one of them really cleaned up the company vehicle last night before they came to work!

The team meetings all start on time and everybody contributes. There might be a little bit of disagreement because they have different views, but we're all here for the same cause.

The customers ring and say what a great team you've got, and how they enjoyed the performance of the team.

The team performance is consistent, and you know that when you send the team to do something it will be done how you expect. Oh yea!

When there is a challenge, someone takes ownership of it and there's a frank discussion about how to do better next time.

When you need a new team member, because you are such a great place to work, one of your existing team brings someone along who they recommend. The costs within the business are consistent and predictable because you know exactly what's going to happen with your biggest resource - your team.

The communication between you and your clients or customers is at the level of a partnership: *we're all going forward in this together*.

You know the holiday that you're planning for three weeks will be a great time, and there is no stress because you know you'll be coming back to a better situation than you're leaving.

Once again you should have a vision of, a picture of the utopia or the end game you want for your team. After many years of coaching business owners and working with businesses, I've found that number ten above - the idea of going away for three or four weeks on a holiday and coming back to something that is better - really frames the dream. SO, Step 1 - Really define your desire.

Step 2 - Have a plan

There is an old saying, that "*Rome wasn't built in a day*". And there isn't time here or now to do a customised thirty-page plan on how to improve your four teams. (That's the kind of work I do 1:1 with clients). But if you don't spend ten minutes on the worksheet at the back of this book just working out a few fundamentals of how you're going to change what you're doing, then this opportunity for success will be severely diminished.

It doesn't take a rocket scientist to realise that: yes, we want Reliability, Consistency and Engagement across our four teams. But the four teams are dramatically different usually in what they want from us. So there has to be a slightly different approach or a slightly different set of actions with each of your four teams.

One of the cool things you have to plan to do, is think how you're going to communicate or tell people around you (members of your team), that you will be trying to change what you're doing.

A bit of a strategy here in communication is needed.

You can use the worksheets at the end of the book to come up with some ideas or methodology and a timeline for putting this in place.

Do not try and do this all-in-one step, all at once, because simply there are too many moving parts.

Start with a simple thing such as a team meeting with an agenda that's followed up, that you do reliably, that you prepare for. You may use a mentor to assist you with this. You may use a friend who's done this before. But the mere fact that you are having a team meeting and you are reliable, and you are communicating with your team will mean they will be more engaged.

Once again, change doesn't happen overnight, but it does happen. As you go down the track of (for example) having team meetings, if your desires are for a Reliable, Consistent, Engaged team, then your team meetings must be reliable. That is, at the same time every week. They must be consistent, so you must have an agenda and follow up the actions from the agenda.

And they must be engaging. So, you must do a little bit of preparation, and follow through on the action-points that are the outcomes of the meeting. The more you desire the team to be successful, and the more passionate and enthusiastic you are in making this work, the easier it will be for your teams to follow you.

People follow people who are passionate and enthusiastic. The step you have to take is to be enthusiastic about the changes you are making and really drive those forward.

As an example of enthusiasm, imagine if you rang one of your core suppliers and asked for a meeting to discuss how you can improve your business with them. You can look at the profitability for both of your businesses and look at the forecast you have in the next say six months about your purchases and your desires to make your business better. And how the two of you working together can do Better Business.

I suggest strongly that your supplier would not only make themselves available for the meeting, but would also probably make coffee because they are enthusiastic about doing business with you because you are their client.

They make money *from you!*

If you are enthusiastic and passionate about growing your business, and growing your business with them, then they will simply want to be involved.

If they don't want to be involved, then there's a whole raft of decisions you have to make about "*actually is this a supplier you wish to be associated with*?" But that's a whole new and different discussion.

So, Step two: make a Plan.

Step 3: The Resistance

Because this might be a little bit new to you or your suppliers, your clients, and your personal support network, or more specially your team at work, you will get resistance.

The resistance comes purely from a place of fear.

FEAR: False Expectations Appearing Real.

Nearly all human beings fear change; that is: the unknown.

Your teams may fear the change because the results of the change are not visible to them yet.
They may fear the change because you've said this sort of thing before. They may fear the change because they've been in environments or with people who have talked about trying to change things before.

DESIRE + PLAN

MUST BE GREATER THAN RESISTANCE

What you have to be absolutely consistently focused on, is that the outcomes of four teams working together are better for everybody. Your clients get better supply of goods and better performance of services when your suppliers are involved. Your home team has a less stressful environment when things go right and when you as the pivot central person are happy, at rest, and spend less time at work and are more successful.

So, your desire and your plan must be demonstrated with enthusiasm, passion, and consistency.

By telling the people in the teams what you are doing, where you're going and why, it will bring them on board a lot easier. At the end of the book in the worksheets there are a couple of ideas about communicating with the four teams. And never ever be afraid to ask for feedback.

The bottom line is that every person wants to be more successful and wants to have a better life. So, by telling people *"this is what we're doing"*, then they will come on board a lot better.

Your desire plus your plan must be bigger than the resistance you are going to get. Then you have certainty to make it work.

So, this is a really simple three-step formula for change:

Desire + Plan > Resistance

Chapter six

USING YOUR VALUES

Think through, Decide, Own and Model YOUR Behaviours and Values.

I remember working with a business owner, on the performance of his business and his team.

I sat in various team meetings while he berated and critiqued the people in the meeting for not finishing their paperwork on time and not being accurate in the detailing that was required. The net effect of this was that the invoicing for the company could not be done in a just-in-time fashion, and obviously this had cashflow implications. This was a huge, amazing frustration to the owner of the business.

What interested me most was that the owner himself was the worst offender for filling out or detailing the worksheets and paperwork that were needed to show completion of various work that the company did.

Often on the fourth or fifth working day of the following month, I would be asking why revenue was down, only to be told by the administrator that the owner had yet to finish invoicing, reports, and/or government compliance requirements that enabled them to invoice.

On pointing this out to the business owner, he looked at me incredulously and told me he was busy and that other things took priority over doing this paperwork.

My question was really simple:
"So, you expect your team to do this, but you don't live by this rule that the job isn't finished till the paperwork is done?".

This is a direct and absolute example of not modeling the behaviours or the values you expect from your team.

If you desire change, and you desire to have a better team, the first thing you must do is decide and agree with yourself the values and behaviours you are going to define, agree and display.

If you expect honesty, reliability, consistency, and engagement then you must firstly model these before you can expect them.

The management or leadership maxim to "lead from the front" comes to mind.

There are over 100 universally agreed and or available values which you can find online. But these can usually be brought down to half a dozen keywords. For the purposes of this book, we are distilling all these values and behaviours down to three: Consistency, Reliability and Engagement.

"When you lead by values it does not cost your business; it helps your business". **Jerry Greenfield.**

The link between values and behaviours is very simple. Your behaviours are tangible and visible evidence of your values. This is not some soft saying - this is true! The values that you decide you wish to display and model will be reflected in the behaviours that you have. Your behaviour with your team will become the behaviours that the team display.

"Behaviour is the mirror in which everyone shows their image." **Johann Goeth.**

So, the values and behaviours we want from our teams are Reliability, Consistency and Engagement.

As the leader of the teams, you have to lead with these three behaviours and enjoy, model, demonstrate and live these three values.

In the book *"The Leadership Challenge"* by Kouzes and Posner, they talk about behaviour and credibility.

6 elements of great leadership

To be a great leader to lead great teams, there are six short phrases that come to mind:

1. Practice what you preach
2. Walk the talk
3. Your actions are consistent with your words
4. You put your money where your mouth is
5. You follow through on your promises
6. You do what you say you will do.

So, let's put some thought in and spend some time on this as a business owner.

What values are really important to you, personally? Because your personal values will be reflected in your business values. You can't hide from your personal values and behaviours.

Common values

Here are some common values that business owners often start with:

- Honesty
- Pride
- Accountability
- Courage
- Ambition
- Respect
- Ownership
- Consistency
- Reliability

- Loyalty
- Equality
- Engagement
- Wisdom
- Spirituality.

This is not a full or comprehensive list. It is just a starting place to begin thinking about which values are important to you. There is a free online value assessment tool at **www.personalvalu.es**

This is a free little values checklist. You could do the quiz on this website, bearing in mind that you have your own history and thought patterns. But it does make you think about what is important to you, which is a good first step.

Once you have defined the 4-6 key values that are most important to you, then you need to start thinking about how these transmit. How will these be transcribed and demonstrated in the business?

The key to the success of your four teams, is how will you model these values and behaviours in your business. Because this is the behaviour, the values and the performance that all of your teams will follow. What you model is what you will receive.

As an example: Reliability.

If you judge Reliability to be an imperative to your business, to your team and therefore, the success of your venture, is this what you display and model? Can it be said that you are never late for meetings? Can it be said that you always turn up on time and follow through on what you say you will do? Can it be said that when you make an appointment to turn up on a job, you turn up on that job at that time? Are your reports and paperwork done as you would expect them to be, as your clients as your suppliers expect, and as your staff would expect them to be?

These are some of the pillars of reliability that you expect from your team. If they see that you do not display them, or model them, then realistically they will not adopt them as their behaviours.

Don't hide your values or your success behaviours. Pay the very few dollars and get someone to do a graphic of these values and put them on the wall in the office. Put them on the front page of your website. Put on the bottom of your invoices:

"We as a company believe in these values"
because this will hold you to account not only from yourself, but from your other team members, your suppliers, your clients and your staff members.

As with all behaviours and values, the results are in the eye of the beholder. What this means is that your definition of "reliable" might not be the same as your clients' or your suppliers' or your staff team's definition of reliable. One of the secrets to our being successful, is to have an agreed set of values, an agreed set of behaviours.

Communication about these values is the start to the agreement of how we will behave, and how we will judge and model this value.

As an example: you make an appointment for 2:00 PM and while you are on the way to the appointment, there is an accident on the motorway, and you are delayed. It is possibly unreasonable for the other party to perceive that you are unreliable when you could not help the delay.

But, did you call the other party as soon as you realised there was a delay and explain? Did you think of using technology to have the meeting remotely while you were stuck on the side of the road? What were the possible and reasonable actions you could have taken to make the meeting work?

The core of how strong you believe in your values, your behaviours and how you model both, is when you are under stress or when the unforeseeable happens. This is when, as the owner of the business or the leader, you stand up and make decisions that are aligned to the core of what you do; to what you believe and who you are. This is when your behaviours and values align to model and prove you are Reliable, Engaged and Consistent.

Thinking about how your team behaves, it's easy for them to be Reliable, Consistent and Engaged when the ship is sailing smoothly. But you as a business owner want them to be these three things all the time. It is when the challenge comes on, the situations change, or you must make decisions that the truth of your modeling and the truth of your values comes to the fore.

When working with your teams, paint a picture - a clear picture - with your modeling and behaviours.

Using the example about being delayed heading to a meeting:

1. Are you the one who made a phone call 30 minutes before the meeting advising the other attendees that you'd be late and sharing why?

2. Are you the one who contacted another team member who was closer to the meeting to attend in your absence, fully briefing them by phone on the way to the meeting while you sat on the side of the road?

3. Are you the one that said: "Look, can we have this meeting on Zoom now"?

4. Are you the one that accepted responsibility for the delay and made it work?

This is an interesting question because, if this was a team member stuck on the side of the road, would you as the business owner see their subsequent actions as reliable? That is a situation out of their control, but they really tried to make it work. Or did their best to make it work.

Are they, or you, modeling Consistency, Reliability and Engagement?

Understanding that your values and behaviours will influence the performance of your team is key to becoming a great team leader.

Chapter seven

HOW TO GET YOUR 4 TEAMS TO BE RELIABLE

Reliability

What is reliability?

Reliability: *the probability that a product system will serve, will perform its intended function adequately for a specified period of time, and operate in a defined environment without failure.*

Or in real terms for people:

Do what you say you will do when you say you will do it.

Simple really!!

Let's call the things that people are doing when they are reliable **success behaviours**.

If there's one thing that drives society or business success, it is the behaviours that people constantly display. Their success behaviours. The commonly accepted things that people do that lead to a good result; that lead to clients being happy; that lead to all parties knowing what to expect. That is what to reliably expect.

Different societies, businesses, and teams will have different expectations of the behaviour that may be displayed at various times. They will all define reliability differently. They may have defined explanations of how they see these things, how these things are measured and how they are rewarded. But we all have these success behaviours.

If we think about societal behaviour and reliability, then at times it is quite unique. You might think of something called *Island time*. How often have we been traveling through the Pacific islands maybe for a holiday, and we've been to a meal or a meeting, we've arrived on time and the other people for the meeting have arrived late or the meals have been a little bit delayed. It's a variable thing and sometimes in the islands they call it *Island time*. It's not a reliability thing - it's just for them that time has a different rhythm.

We are going to break our discussion about Reliability into three areas:

- Define Reliability
- Will and Pride
- Feedback.

Define reliability in your world.

It is true that behaviours make the person.

As a business owner or leader in the community, or as a leader in your own team or your own home, your behaviour is the example others follow. As mentioned earlier, your behaviours are based on your **values**.

You cannot expect your company, your family, or your society to be well-disciplined, well-focused or reliable if it's not how you behave. If it's not what you model or expect.

Just as we expect good and successful behaviours from others around us, we have a raft of behaviours that we will *not* accept.

All human behaviours sit in somewhat of a continuum:

- those that we love and really wish to encourage

- those that we indulge or put up with due to circumstances; and

- those we will not accept and effectively wish that at that point we want to terminate the relationship.

The definitions of behaviours that are encouraged, acceptable and desired is imperative. **Reliability** is the first success behaviour that we have to define.

My definition of Reliability:

To say what you are going to do; to do what you say you are going to do with your best effort; and achieve the expected result.

This is what every business owner wants from every one of his teams.

They want Reliability as a fact.

And the behaviour in the business needs to be agreed and aligned with what in this particular circumstance and team in the business needs.

From working with many business owners and many business teams, a simple question I ask is: *What does Reliability mean to you*?

The simple question brings a raft of different answers. These answers are usually based on personal history, personal employment experiences and often cultural and family influences.

An individual's definition of Reliability is often based on the importance that they placed in their role in the business. That is, how they view the value of their contribution to the success of the business overall.

If they hold the view that they play just a small part or that their part is not important, then their focus on Reliability and on a predictable outcome for them will be impacted by that attitude and that knowledge.

There are some simple solutions to the Reliability alignment quandary:

- Get every member of the team to define what a Reliable team means for them.

- Make sure every member of the team, that is for all four teams, knows how important they are as part of the success for your venture.

- As part of your interview process, your one-on-one meetings, and your review process, reinforce the need for Reliability in all areas of the business.

Reliability, the art of saying what you're going to do and always doing it to your best endeavors, is a key accelerator to success in any business.

___Action Point 1___

Write your own short definition of Reliability

Ask every member of your team to do the same.

The will

As part of your interview process and part of your regular review process with all of your four teams, discussion should be had about the will to be reliable and the will to be working where we are. The will to be reliable and the will to always do your best, is the hallmark of a successful team member, and therefore successful team.

There is a very old and famous saying in recruitment which is:

"recruit for attitude and train aptitude."

If within your team - that is all four of your teams - you have team members who do not have the will, the desire, the attitude, the drive to be reliable, to do their best, to turn up when they say they will be there, and to give of their best at all times, then corrective action, training, motivation and feedback needs to be given.

It is pointless having the best surgeon in the world do an operation on your body if they fail to turn up or turn up late.

Pride is one of the core emotions of reliable delivery:

I'm proud of the uniform I'm wearing; I'm proud of the company I work for; I'm proud of the outcomes that we deliver for our clients and our participants; and I'm proud of what I do as a cog in this wheel to make this happen.

Pride is frequently driven by being part of the greater good. Of contributing to the endeavour in a meaningful way. Thus, you need to ensure that every team member knows that they are a pivotal cog in the machine, and that their contribution is as important as others in the business machine.

One of the four teams we involve ourselves with is our suppliers. Often these suppliers are left out of the end of a project. The supplier may supply a small or seemingly insignificant component for two parts on a project - but without these small building blocks, the project or process cannot be completed.

For the suppliers to be truly part of the four teams that make our business successful, then they need to be as involved as every other person and every other team member in the celebration and the success of the projects that they contribute to. The net result of this is purely that by human nature, they will be interested in the projects going forward as they will be engaged, acknowledged and part of the celebrations when the project is finished.

This can be as simple as sending a set of photos of the finished project or sharing feedback from a client about the quality of the work or the project. Or sending an invitation to view the project when it's finished. It is not the quantity of the acknowledgement; it is about the acknowledgement being done.

We're trying to drive the will to be reliable and have pride in what we're doing, and the pride in doing what we say we're going to do. By acknowledging everybody's part - that is absolutely everybody's part - and getting everybody to share in the success, stress and acknowledgment when the process is finished, we build goodwill to be part of this and pride to be part of the achievement.

Action Point 2

Write down the last two acknowledgements of success you gave to your suppliers

Begin a brag book of photographs at home to review your successes.

Feedback

Reliability without feedback will either be short-lived or not demonstrated at all.

Because Reliability is a success behaviour, we need to acknowledge and give feedback on it frequently.

Reliability forms the backbone of our teams:

- Turning up on time.

- Delivering when you say you're going to deliver it.

Feedback and training has to start at the interview, and be carried on through reviews and meetings. There should be a constant source of acknowledgement at all toolbox meetings with suppliers and discussions with customers.

A simple question to your clients:

We pride ourselves on Reliability - how's your experience been of this?

If indeed everything's been going as a client expected, the process and the project is being done as they expect, then you will get the answer you're looking for.

But if the client does comment:

*"Well actually I was expecting **this** to happen at **this** time."*

Well, here is an opportunity for you to improve the performance of your company out of the process. Feedback is just so valuable.

Only one of two things has happened here: either the client's expectations are not what they should be, and this could be because of previous experience or communication they have had; or your business delivery is not meeting the framework that you gave the client.

This is feedback. This is a training opportunity and a development opportunity for your business and your team.

You can ask the same question of your suppliers, your home team and of your clients.

The question is simple.

We pride ourselves on Reliability - how is your experience of this?

Any feedback is good feedback. Any feedback allows you to either bask in the joy and in the glory of being a reliable supplier in business, or to look at a training or development opportunity for your business or your teams.

Confucius says:

A man who lacks reliability is utterly useless.

Reliability is that vital.

Action Point 3

Ask your home team the reliability question.

Chapter eight

HOW TO GET YOUR 4 TEAMS TO BE CONSISTENT

Consistency noun (BEING THE SAME)

The quality of always behaving or performing in
a similar way, or of always happening in
a similar way:

*They've won a few games this season but
they lack consistency.*

It's important to show some consistency in your work.

The fastest man on the planet, Usain Bolt, clearly knows a thing or two about running.

Reaching speeds of nearly 28mph, Usain Bolt holds the world records at both 100m and 200m. And while we can't all run as fast as Usain, he is adamant that we can improve with the right training, approach and kit.

"If you're not the athletic type," he says, *"it's going to take more to get your body in the shape that you want. But if you really want it, it's possible. It's all about consistency."*

The Rules of the Game

The Key accelerator to achieve Consistency is using the **Rules of the Game.**

In all of life, in every facet, everywhere we work, play and indeed every breath we take, there are rules. These are the "Rules of the Game".

One of the best ways to think of Rules of the Game is to put it into a sporting context.

As an example, most of us know the rules of football. One of the simple rules that is easy to understand is *handball*: that is, you're not allowed to play the ball with your hand.

Let us imagine a game of football on the beach.

There are two teams: four or five of one family, and five or so members from another family. They are having a social game of football on the beach. As the ball is kicked around and everyone laughs and has a good time, the ball is touched by the hand of one of the young people in one of the teams. The referee - a father with a hooter - just lets the game carry on because after all, they are here to have a good time and we're playing on the beach. And the last thing we want is to make the rules get in the way of a great game on the beach.

Now later that afternoon, you go and watch a First Eleven game of football between two intensely competitive high schools. There is a referee who's qualified and authorised, with a whistle and a little book in his back pocket. The game is played with intensity, pace and skill.

And at that pivotal moment, one of the players touches the ball with his hand. The referee blows shrilly on the whistle and it is a free kick. It is a direct free kick at the goal by the other team. A direct result of the handball. A goal is scored.

Now lastly, think about watching a football game between two world class teams: let's say, England playing Germany. As the game is played, you see the intensity of the rules, the authority of the referee, and the technical juggernaut behind the referee with video replays etc.

The ball is kicked, and a player touches it with his hand. The referee deems it to be deliberate, so there is a free kick and a yellow card. It is watched on the big screen by the 80,000 people that are at the stadium, and by the millions watching it online. The player gets a yellow card, and the ramifications for the team are huge. A goal is scored and the team are out of the World Cup.

OK. Here's the thing.

The interesting thing here is every person from the people on the beach, through to the parents and the players of First Eleven football game, and the international players/viewers know that "you can't touch the ball with your hand". This rule has not changed in hundreds of years. What has changed is the adherence to the rule, the ramifications of breaking the rule, and the technology or reporting available around the rule and the consistent application of the rule.

To put it simply; the rules remain the same. But the more intense we are on these AGREED rules, the more we obey our rules, the more we have our rules in writing and look to them for guidance, the higher the standard will be of performance of the players or team.

Consistent adherence to, observation of and an understanding of the rules and the ramifications of breaking these rules, drive the players to perform better.

In business, Rules of the Game are an imperative to a high performing business, a high performing team - and what is more, to a happy business and a happy engaged team. The more agreed the rules are and the more consistently they are applied, the better the outcomes will be for all parties.

The better everybody knows the rules, the better everybody understands the rules, the better everybody is trained across the rules and understands the ramifications and intentions of them, the better the performance of the business and the teams.

Let's break our *Rules of the Game* approach to Consistency into seven accelerators for change:

1. Definition of Rules

2. Agreement from all

3. Constant outcomes

4. Review

5. Visibility

6. Consequences

7. Recognition

We're going to look at each of these accelerators now, to see how you can use this approach to increase the Consistency of your teams.

Definition of the Rules.

The clearer and more defined the rules are, the easier they are to follow and enforce, and the easier they are to understand.

As soon as rules have any ambiguity or grey areas, then this is the area where the poor performers and the people who want to make excuses go.

Simplicity and clarity are imperative for good rules.

Remember the KISS principle: **Keep It Simple Stupid**. Make all rules clear and simple.

As a sample rule:
The start time in the office is 8:00 AM.
This is definite, absolutely clear, simple and concise. Which makes it understandable and enforceable.

It is important to not have rules, just for rules' sake. But there must be enough rules to cover all circumstances, and within reason all outcomes.

There is a saying "*the exception proves the rule*". What this means is that in exceptional circumstances in business as in life, and as in sport, the rules can be bent or broken. But this will be the exception.

Within the rules, the definition should also give as much clarity as is required to ensure no ambiguity: *All staff shall wear corporate dress at all times.* This is an example of what could be considered a loose rule.

All staff shall wear corporate dress which shall be cleaned, freshly laundered and appropriate at all times.

This is a better example of the same rule. We are only using a few more words to offer clarity and to remove ambiguity.

Action Point 1.

Start with writing a list of the situations in your business where you would like to have rules. At this point it does not have to be long.

Write a few simple rules for each of the four teams.

Here are some thought starters:

- *Staff team - Start time? Internet usage at work? Cellphones at work?*
- *Clients - Payment term? Availability? Authorisations for variances?*
- *Suppliers – Communication frequency? Deliveries?*
- *Home Team - Time at work? After hours phone calls?*

Remember to start simple and try and think through what you as a business owner or leader want to achieve in your business.

With four teams, a lot of the rules of the game will be common across every team - Timeliness, Honesty, Communication, etc. And remember the simpler, the clearer the rules are, the better the performance between the teams.

Agreement from all.

I had a client in legal services a little while ago, who decided that because it was his business, he would set the Rules of the Game and the agreement would come from the enforcement of the rules.

The most telling outcome of his approach came from his clients or his customers, who just refused to be told the rules that they had to agree to, in order to trade with him. After discussion, none of the clients objected to the terms of trade, the payment terms or the changes - but to be told rankles. To be *involved* enlightens.

It is pointless having Rules of the Game if every person involved does not know what the rules are.

Imagine if the people playing soccer on the beach thought that the other people were playing rugby!

Equally important is that every member of the team has to agree that these Rules of the Game are the rules that they wish to abide by. Once again, if you think of a sporting situation, if someone in the football team decided they wanted to use their hands then this would be a problem.

Working with a number of business owners over the last few years, I have found that the easiest way to get agreement on Rules of the Game is to have a dedicated staff meeting around this subject.

What we have found is that usually most of the team know the rules. For example, what time they should start work, and when reports are due.

The meeting about Rules of the Game is to put these rules into a formal environment. That is, *"these are the rules that we are going to run our team by"*.

As new team members come on board, you should give them a copy in writing of Rules of the Game:

"this is how we run our business; this is how we run our operation".

If you think of how you deal with your clients, these Rules of the Game are usually found in your terms of trade. Or in the terms of trade you have with your suppliers.

> *Action Point 2.*
>
> *Organise and arrange a quick meeting with your staff, to discuss and agree rules of the game going forward.*
>
> *Organise and arrange a quick one-on-one meeting with a couple of suppliers, to discuss and agree Rules of the Game going forward.*

Constant outcomes

The rationale behind Rules of the Game is to have constant outcomes. So, any rules that do not drive towards or accelerate towards a constant and consistent outcome need to be clarified, modified, and rewritten.

When setting up Rules of the Game, we need to be absolutely sure that if we follow all of these rules and perform our tasks well, that we will get a successful outcome.

A great example of this is a sales process. In a business your sales process starts from the first contact with the client. So, rules around how the phone is answered, how the client is dealt with, and the information the client is sent, should be detailed in your Rules of the Game. If you follow these rules, you should move the client to the next level - that is, from a phone call to a visit to a quote, etc.

At home, you may set up a rule where you get a defined couple of hours to do office stuff without interruption. This gives you time to really focus and sets up expectations about how important this time is.

Action Point 3.

Look at one rule you have written for the workplace. Think of the outcome that this rule is designed to achieve. Now make sure that you have all the clarity, steps and all the process is in place to do this.

Now repeat the first bullet point for one home team rule.

Review

As with all other things in business, all the Rules of the Game should be reviewed frequently. As you receive feedback from the other teams, this will give you a way you can develop and improve the rules.

The question should be asked:

"Is this rule getting us the consistent results that we want right now?"

A great example of this was in April of 2020 when we were in the middle of the COVID crisis. Rules of the Game around turning up to work, what you wore, and dealing with clients changed dramatically. And the companies that reviewed, refreshed and wrote a new set of rules for operation, succeeded to a far greater extent than those that did not.

A change in the market, movement by competition, or a success in some area - these are a few of the examples of drivers for a review of rules.

Action Point 4.

What rules of the game for your business changed in 2020? What could you have done differently or more effectively had you changed or morphed more quickly?

Visibility

Every member of the team must have visibility of the outcomes of breaches of the rules. In a sports ground, the reason for the coloured card is so that everybody can see what is going on.

There has to be the ability to see and then act on rules that are broken. Rules that are invisible or cannot be validated or enforced are of little use.

Visibility also allows the manager or leader an opportunity to train, improve performance, or modify the actions of that team member to improve both the company performance and the relationship.

I've worked with a few clients that have had debtor challenges - that is, people who owe them money. We have found that if you can sit with the client and work through the cash challenge (the debt), then not only do you resolve that problem, but during that meeting you can work through a set of new Rules of the Game so that this does not happen again.

Everybody has an understanding of the discussion; everybody is in agreement and we move on.

Much the same when an employee is late to work. It is usually not only the owner or manager that notice, because often extra work or stress falls on other team members.

From a communication and involvement POV it is really important that the team members who are impacted know that you, as the owner or manager, are looking at this and working on this. Obviously, the discussion between you and the staff member is between you and the staff member only. But visibility for others that something is being done is imperative.

Action Point 5.

Make a note of how you do currently, or how you would report on the rules in ACTION POINT 1

Consequences

In the case of my legal services client, once we had agreement from their clients then we were able to vastly improve the company's cash flow by reminding clients we were just adhering to our new agreed terms of trade.

Now that you have the rules, you must decide the consequences. If you think of the sporting example: when you break one of the rules, there is a consequence - a penalty, a colored card, etc.

When a rule is broken, the consequence must match the ramifications of breaking the rule. And obviously if the rule continues to be broken, then there are only one of two outcomes: the first is that the rule needs to be reviewed; the second is that the person who continues to break the rule must have a deeper consequence for this continued breach.

This is one of the more difficult parts of implementing the Rules of the Game.

To be clear, if everybody at the front of this discussion agrees to the Rules of the Game, then they are agreeing that there will be a ramification or a consequence to breaking the rule.

Just as in football, a handball in the middle of the field is a free kick. A handball in the penalty area is a penalty.

So, when a Rule of the Game is broken, the situation, the intensity, and the intent all have to be taken into account before a consequence is put in place.

We need to be mindful that the consequences will drive further behaviour. There is an opportunity with every Rule of the Game to have a set of consequences that retrain, remotivate and re-engage the team member.

As an example, a Team member may be constantly late with reporting or finishing documentation for work done.

An approach may be to tell the person again and again that it is late but not acceptable etc.

A second approach may be to point out to the team member that the failure to do this work or provide this report holds up another part of the business process. For example, invoicing if it was information about a job or work, or management decisions if it is a report.

A third approach might be to ask the team member what you as the owner or manager need to do to make sure that this report or work arrives on time as it is imperative to what else you have to do in the business.

If this is not the first occurrence of this breach, dated notes should be kept and this should be reminded to the person in this discussion.

One of the core benefits of having a Rules of the Game approach is the ability to often have a positive, proactive and re-engaging outcome.

Remember that Rules of the Game are initially set and agreed by the team after consultation. It is expected that the reports are on time and that these will be delivered so that the right management decisions can be made.

Thinking of the above example where someone is late with a report or late with some paperwork - when there *is* a change in delivery of the paperwork or a change in attitude that gets it done on time, there is an opportunity here to praise the person. To praise the person in front of the team or to tell the person the positive difference that this has made to you in the business.

And from a training and development point of view, often an explanation of how imperative this particular task is to the business process, the business sales, or profit will further reinforce the actions, the behaviours, the Rules of the Game.

The consequences of breaking the rules, is a process or discussion and the consequences of moving to the rules and abiding by them is praise and a better working environment. So you can in fact turn any non-adherence to the rules into an opportunity to share a bit more with that team member about why that rule is important, and engage them further.

Obviously, the consequences must reflect both the seriousness and the frequency of the breach of the rules. And one of the key aspects of the Rules of the Game is that all team members across the four teams must have amazing visibility and transparency of the journey that will be embarked upon should Rules of the Game continue to be broken.

There are certain Rules of the Game that once broken will be terminal for the relationship. Once again, this has to be spelt out at the initial start of the relationship with any of the four teams. Some examples are:

- Clients who repeatedly do not pay their accounts on time.
- Suppliers who do not supply the quality goods you have ordered in a just-in-time fashion.
- Possibly the home support team who gives you no time to think about what you need to do for your business.
- Dishonesty, aggression, abuse, or disrespect in the workplace.

Once again, it does depend on the seriousness and the frequency of the breach.

But Rules of the Game are just that.

And if you want to play this game, be clear, be strong; then these are the rules.

The importance of absolute adherence to Rules of the Game for high performance cannot be overstated.

An example of this is being late to the office or to the workplace. Not only is this disrespectful, stressful to the other workers, and at times very stressful to the business owner for workflow and work management, it is breaking a basic rule of human endeavour.

So, this is an example of a rule that has to be spelt out at the interview and reinforced at the team meetings. And the consequences you put in place for your rule around being late, should reflect the potential impact of this behaviour on the business.

Action Point 6.

Think of a Rule of the Game that you perceive is broken in your workplace. What are two possible consequences? You should have one that is for an initial instance of the rule being broken, and a second consequence for a continual failure to follow that rule.

Then, think how would you put in place a retraining regime or an opportunity for you to improve the person's performance in this case?

Recognition

Every human being strives to be successful.

Different teams and different individuals have different expectations of what success means.

But recognition is pivotal, as an emotional hook it maintains engagement.

It is no coincidence that the most successful companies in the world have a huge focus on recognition. Employee of the month, most improved employee, best salesperson, most improved function engineer. Recognition is the key to hooking the emotions.

Being able to recognise, reward and celebrate outstanding performance is one of the best parts of Rules of the Game.

Having a team member in any team that stands by the rules, works with the rules and really gives you good feedback on the rules is a great resource for you and your company.

Because your rules are simple and clear, it is easy to keep a framework where you reward people. All human beings like praise, and reward in front of your peers or indeed your industry is a great motivator.

Recognition, like consequences, has to be in line with each rule.

Idea: if you had a work team of eight who previously had a challenged arrival time, and then after a short meeting (about the importance of timeliness) were at work on time every workday for a month - would we buy them a couple of pizzas for lunch?

Remembering that if we have three teams of eight, then the other two are going to be seeing this. So they may have a go at being less reliable to get pizza or react in another way. So think on this a bit!

Action Point 7

Is there a supplier that you would like to do more business with? What do they have to do, what rule do they have to hold for you to do more with them?

At home if you get the little quiet time you need, how will you make the home team feel part of the success?

Summary of using the Rules of the Game to achieve Consistency:

Remember the management maxim:
INSPECT WHAT YOU EXPECT.

If you have a rule and you make it visible and you give it consequences and rewards, it will improve in its validity and adherence. Thus improving CONSISTENCY and team performance.

SO

Rules of the Game are an imperative for all four teams. An agreement and a commitment to what we're trying to achieve, the consequences if we don't achieve it, and the recognition of celebration when we do. This will earn you an amazing way of engaging, motivating and involving all the members of your team.

Within the work environment, Rules of the Game are simply the actions, behaviours, end outcomes we expect from the people who are tasked with doing the job.

From a simple script on how we answer the phone – *"this is how we answer the phone*; *we always answer the phone this way"* - through to reporting, how we deal with customers, how we deal with our stock. The Rules of the Game are pivotal in every area of the business.

They must be written down, agreed and every member of the team has to make a commitment to make sure this happens. And understand the consequences if it doesn't.

Every new staff member should be aware of the Rules of the Game. Often a lot of these are carried out or carried forward in SOPs, or standard operating procedures. But Rules of the Game are much simpler, tighter, and more basic than that.

And the more basic, more "Lego block-like" they are, the more people will understand them. The easier they are to commit to and have consequences for.

Within the teams that form your suppliers and your clients, Rules of the Game are vital. How you communicate around your terms of trade, your expectations of price, your payment terms, and every part of that interaction has to be part of your set of rules.

Too often in business, the terms of engagement between a company and its clients, a company and its suppliers are at best, *what is understood at the time*. As soon as a grey area appears, there will at some stage be trouble.

Simply the more detail, the more time, the more effort, the more understanding, the more agreement on your Rules of the Game, the better the relationship will remain for a very long time.

Once you have agreed Rules of the Game, then everybody knows exactly what playing field we are on.

It is much the same in your fourth support team - your home team. Often within a business environment you may not tell your support team about various areas of the business. But this is as much a Rule of the Game as the actual rules. That is, people and team members need to know what they're not being told, so that we are working in a no-surprises environment.

Rules of the Game understood by all parties are an absolute imperative to being Consistent.

Consistent communication, consistent performance, and consistent outcomes give everybody a far greater enjoyment going forward.

Chapter nine

HOW TO GET YOUR 4 TEAMS TO BE ENGAGED

ENGAGEMENT

You MUST - you simply have to - Lead

Leadership, a noun - *the action of leading a group of people or an organisation.*

My definition of the difference between a manager and a leader is:

The **manager** gets information and assists to make the decision for the organisation to achieve its goals after checking information. If the information is sound and the decision is made, then the organisation is on the right track.

The **Leader** takes information, adds the dimension of the team, then makes a decision. The team that is expected to achieve these goals, achieve these outcomes. The leader is thinking: *how do I get the best from, the best for and contribute the best to the team?*

There have been more books, articles and columns of print dedicated to the subject of leadership then any one person could possibly read in a lifetime. In fact, in my small business library I have dozens of books on leadership.

Some talk of the qualities of a leader: sacrifice, style, communication efforts. Hundreds of leaders such as the ill-fated Robert Falcon Scott through to Bill Gates, Richard Branson, Bill Clinton, and All Black Captain Kieran Read. There is much to be read, much to be learned, and much to be waded through, absorbed, and thought about.

Leadership - an imperative accelerator to your four Teams. And the most important aspect of leadership that you need to achieve is for your four teams to be Engaged.

Let's break leadership for Engagement into seven thoughts:

- **Desire**
- **Honesty**
- **Knowledge and learning**
- **Common goals**
- **Action Plans**
- **Huddles and One on Ones**
- **Rituals.**

Desire

For me, the first core need for a great leader is desire. The desire to *be* a leader. The desire to want the organisation or team or group to succeed at a level that they possibly have not previously.

Desire leads to positivity, and by default people follow positive people. There are hundreds of books written about the impact of positivity and optimism on teams. It is true: no one follows or listens to a "negative Nelly "!

Positivity leads to a drive to make things happen. This drive to make things happen leads to a drive for research and for innovation. The drive to make an organisation great. This obviously has an impact on the energy levels and activity levels of the team. Great drive for their organisation is tangible with a positivity and energy that is amazing. What great evidence of engagement!

Desire goes to positivity and this is demonstrated by the will. The will to do the extra bit, the will to listen to all other people, the will to be a part of what's going on - and the will to be a great leader. If indeed you have the desire to be a leader, the second thing you must have after positivity is confidence. Confidence not only in yourself, but confidence in the outcome. And the right sense or belief that what you are doing is good and right, and that the organisation and the team of people around you can definitely achieve what you want them to achieve.

In all four Teams, everyone is looking for "a leader". And you do not have to always be the one with the secret or the solution. The desire to lead, drives commitment and energy.

The confidence that your history, your team's history and the organisation's history will give you the experience and the energy you need to achieve the goals you want.

The third part of desire is the ability to dream.

The ability to dream announces you as a leader.

To have the ability to set goals, and within the goals, to have a plan. Because the last thing you want to be as a leader, is leading your team down a path where there is no achievable goal. A good leader will communicate the goals to the teams and know that these goals are achievable with the team they have.

You want to develop the team. You want to educate the team and reward the team. But the dream must be to get to the goals, with a really transparent plan and amazing desire.

Within desire comes resilience. Every leader has to show resilience in the face of adversity. It's the leader who pulls the troops together on the goal line after a goal has just been scored against them and re-focuses the team.

It's the leader who calls a team together who have spent hours completing the project and congratulates them on the quality of the quote work that has been done - in spite of the fact they did not win the job.

But it is also the leader who reminds what needs to be done to win, to win the game, to win the job, to win in the face of adversity.

A leader has a desire, the confidence to lead, ability to communicate to make it happen, and the knowledge through experience and emotional intelligence to lead the team – this is what Engagement looks like.

There is a saying that:

"the squeaky wheel gets the most oil. "

A good leader, a great leader, realises where they should be putting their efforts to achieve team Engagement.

We can measure team engagement against the outcomes we're trying to get from the business. Measure effort against outcomes - against your plan, goals and the KPIs. Because numbers never lie. When you humanize the exception, you allow human intervention, and this is where a great leader will shine. The good leader will allow the percentage of time it takes to get a great outcome with the particular human being involved.

Action Point 1.

Name the best international leader you can.

Give them points out of 10 for desire.

Honesty

Remember Hamish from Chapter One? Well, I remember having a conversation with him about his business. And about how much his good lady knew about the stress he was under. He looked at me and said he did not know how to even start that conversation, because for the past six or seven years he hadn't had any of these conversations with her. I looked back at him and said," *Honesty! Just sit down and start having a short conversation*".

The first conversation will be the hardest, but knowing his wife as I do, I then said to him: "*She will be more concerned about you than about anything you tell her.*"

They now have a monthly date night, where they have a four-minute conversation about the numbers at work. It's about the amount of time it takes the waiter to open a bottle of wine.

Honesty comes in many forms, but the first offshoot of honesty is the ability to communicate. The ability to communicate in a transparent and "no agendas" fashion.

As you are communicating with action plans, goals and dreams - communicate transparently and clearly so that everybody understands exactly what the leader wants. It has to be simple (remember KISS = Keep It Simple Stupid!)

Your communication has to be direct. Great leaders know what they want to say and know how to say it. Using simple words and simple language will make your communication transparent, honest and understandable.

Honesty also comes down to acceptance of difference. All your four teams have different processes, thoughts, experiences, and desired outcomes. So, for every person in the team, whether in a business environment or in a home environment, your communication and message may have to use different language or be varied. The acceptance has to come down to the degree of humanity in leadership. You are leading people. You are leading the human factor. There is an old saying:

"systemise the process; humanize the exception." It is leading the human factor that gets the results that make all the difference in the world. In every successful human endeavour, there is a story of great leadership which comes down to great acceptance of every part of humanity that we have.

Along with the honesty of communication, acceptance of the humanity has to be leadership humility. Great leaders don't have to tell us they are great leaders. They lead, we see them leading, we see them out the front, we see them doing the hours, we see them delivering the results.

Within the four teams, honesty in the leader is an imperative. As people within the four teams will talk to each other, and a story told in one place will reinvent itself or reappear in another.

That's not to say that honesty is not situational. When dealing with the four teams, the information that is given must suit the purpose and the audience to which you're giving it.

An example would be a client who has not paid his account:
The discussion with the client on the impact this is having on your business cash flow is honest and real and should be had.

There may be a need to have an honest and upfront discussion with your suppliers. Because if your client has not paid their account, you may be in a situation where you do not have the cash to pay your supplier's account. Indeed, this is the best way to develop a relationship with your suppliers, to keep them in the loop about what is happening if it is a challenge.

For your work team for the sake of motivation, morale, and certainty in the workplace, it may be ill-advised to tell the team that there is no cash this month. Although it would be leading the team to tell them that this month was tight, and we had to watch our expenses. You could speak to the purchasing Department about holding back on capital purchases and or non-required purchases for the month. Obviously, those within the business that have to know should know, but remember human beings hate uncertainty. And if your business has cash flow problems, then you may bring into play uncertainty with your team at work.

Within the fourth team that is at home, some methodology has to be developed where major cash issues are discussed or at least flagged before they create major mayhem. In my experience, business owners who are under cash stress are sometimes a slightly changed person at home from when things are going along wonderfully.

Action Point 2.

Think through a sticky communication you have had with a team member. How might you have handled it better using honest communication?

What would be another way to approach clients who are constantly late paying?

Knowledge and Learning

While we can wax on lyrically about industry knowledge, knowledge of the market, and knowledge of the way the business should progress, this is just one part of the knowledge circle that a great leader who is engaging their teams requires.

We can put this sort of knowledge loosely into the *experience* category. Experience comes from time on the job, time working in the environment, or time working in the industry. It may be supported by a qualification. This may be formal through University or informal through years working in this or another company.

The best proof of knowledge for a leader is social proof. That is proof from other people that you have the knowledge. Proof that you can be asked questions and provide answers, and that you can be a leader in your field.

It is not essential that the knowledge is at the highest level of the company, as great leaders can glean knowledge from anywhere and facilitate contribution.

Great leaders can demonstrate an amazing amount of emotional IQ. The proven ability to operate in a social environment is usually pivotal to a great leader. This does not mean that the leader has to be the hub of all social attention, and proof of working in a social environment is not necessarily what is the social norm.

Specifically, this kind of knowledge is the ability to communicate to a group of people, to influence a group of people with good discussion, and to have an opinion that is both reasonable, provable, and persuasive to your peers and teams.

This knowledge will also be across methodologies of communication. There are many methods to get your point across. A good leader will have great control of all of them, whether it's verbal, written, in the form of email or a letter. Or it may be a casual discussion, a formal meeting, or presentation.

Good leaders have the ability to positively communicate the dream that is the go-forward of the company. They can pass on their knowledge to a group or an individual so that the group or individual believes that this is the person they should be following: *this is the leader.*

If we agree that part of knowledge is experience, industry knowledge, and social proof of this, and that we have to prove that we can communicate with all levels of people, the next part of provable knowledge is the ability to be flexible.

Flexibility is the ability to change, pivot, and accommodate people and situations around you when it is not exactly according to plan. You have to show the ability to listen, to glean all of the information that you need, and to bring it all together, to allow you and everyone around you who may have some better knowledge areas than you to make the right decisions.

Flexibility and social experience give the leader the opportunity to communicate what the challenges are, and to get the right decision.

While this pillar of engagement leadership is knowledge, it is imperative to realise that as the leader or owner, you don't actually have to have all of the knowledge. One massive strength of a good business owner or leader is the ability and honesty to realise that they don't know the answer/have the knowledge. But the secret is to know where to go to get that information.

Knowledge is a resource that must be constantly developed. It is not by chance that people who we may think of as "professionals" (doctors, accountants, lawyers, pilots) all have to do a solid level of ongoing professional development.

To be engaged, there must be the opportunity to grow, to be developed, to learn.

Part of any ongoing plan or team ideal must be development, learning and growth. Boredom is a major enemy of engagement!

Every team member and every team should have a visible and achievable learning and development regime.

In my years working with business owners, the different industries and different market segments and the different processes required for businesses are so many and varied it would be impossible for any one person to be an expert or an authority in them all. The secret is to know where to go to get that information. So, leave your ego at the door and ask questions.

By asking questions, listening to the answers, reviewing the information and then asking for suggestions/ideas/solutions from your teams, you are actually proving yourself to be confident. You are also engaging everyone. So, have desire and be honest about your situation and your knowledge at this point.

An example of this would be in talking to your supplier team to ask them for a different product or a different brand of product to do the same job. The reason for looking for a different product or a different brand might be a quality challenge, a price point, or a different industry need. Never be afraid to ask the question.

Action Point 3.

Think of a supplier that you deal with and the brand of product you buy often. Consider asking the supplier if there is another brand that would do a similar job. There may be a better-quality bias or be a better price point.

With regards to your home team, be brave enough to ask the question: "are you getting enough information so you're comfortable with what's going on in the business?"

What is the development plan for 1 Team member?

Common Goals

SMART Goals - Specific, Measurable, Attainable, Relevant, and Time-bound.

Engagement and common goals go hand in hand. All human beings wish to be successful. That being the case, you can only be successful when you're achieving what you think you should achieve; what you know you can achieve.

This is not saying that someone else should define what makes you successful. This is saying: set the goals together, and as the leader/business owner go towards their goal. Make the goals achievable.

Within the four teams, goals are a really important part of success, communication, motivation, commitment and finally engagement.

As part of the four-team thought and process, every team has to have their own goals. Purely because each of the teams has a different desired outcome. You, your business is the common link, and your goals bind the four teams together.

So you need to be very clear and precise on what your goals are, your timeline to achieve them, and the mini-goals needed to get there.

As you show desire, enthusiasm, passion and knowledge the four teams will come on board and follow you to be a part of the winning team.

Mini-goals are broken down into achievable bite sized pieces that a particular team can achieve. The common goal concept is that all of these mini goals lead to the common goal.

Your Goal framework

Supplier Goals

+

Client Goals

+

→ **YOUR GOALS**

Team Goals

+

Home Goals

For the business, it might be a certain revenue goal and profit goal. But for the four teams it will mean something completely different:

For the participants or your team in the workplace it will mean certainty of a job, the ability to pay their mortgage - possibly a bonus, possibly a new company vehicle.

For the supplier they get revenue and profit, market share, a quantum of sales and a happy client, you.

For your clients this means good service, a job well done, and their needs being met.

For the home team it means an income for yourself, the mortgage being paid, a lot less stress, an ability to celebrate because the business is going well and you're enjoying yourself.

Having goals, common goals and mini goals allows you to do one of the most important things in business and life: that is celebrate the success of getting to a point. With this success, you need to recognise those around you - those members of the team, or those members of the teams that have contributed to the success of what you have done. Goals allow you to set milestones along the way to see how you are tracking. You'll then know that you're in a good place, or you need to do work in some areas of the business.

Dreams and ideas without a plan and goals are just that - dreams and ideas. When you put a plan and goals into place around your dreams and your ideas, then real traction happens, and the teams come on board. Everyone will become very engaged in their success, which drives your success.

As a business coach and consultant, I've spent hundreds of hours with hundreds of businesses setting up accurate, achievable and exciting goals. Then we look to set up the plan to get there, including milestones, tactics and strategies that really show the business leader and the teams the way to go.

Every team can be involved in this planning process. If you're expecting to double your business in a certain area, then imagine the conversation you could have with your supplier. Calling the meeting to show the plans, goals and discuss with them how they can assist you.

I have never come across a supplier who does not want to be involved with a client who wants to double their business.

There are hundreds of books and thousands of articles on setting goals and doing the plan to get there. At the back of the book on the last page, I will be suggesting half a dozen books that might help with this process. It is an exciting process and leads to a huge degree of engagement when you involve the teams in your plans and dreams.

Imagine the discussion with your home team if you talked about what was going on in the business and you positively talked about a two-year plan to double the business. If we get to this point, you could say the whole family could go for a holiday to Hawaii.

With a plan and a goal, some energy, desire and some dedication, you should get there. But even if you miss the goal by a percentage, you could probably improve enough to take the family to Queenstown for a week. Good stuff!

Action Point 4

What is a goal for your business in two years, you would enjoy discussing with your significant other?

What is the goal you could set for your team at work to improve efficiency by say 5%?

Action Plans

If goals are the target and dreams of the future, then action plans are the mechanisms and the vehicle that drive us to where we want to be.

Think of an action plan as the steps, the small blocks that fit together to make the plan work the dream into a reality.

Action plans achieve three great things in your organisation:

1. They provide a road map for the staff member, team member, supplier or at home to see where they are going, when they should be, and exactly what they should be doing. It's clear, it's concise and to-the-point.

2. It allows you as the leader or business owner to see where every member of the team, all four teams, are in relation to the journey. The journey to the common goal. An action plan breaks down

by each person exactly what they have to do to get us all to the end game.

3. It allows you to motivate, train and develop every person in every team. The action plan, because of its very nature, will allow you to look at strengths and work with those and further train on weaknesses or areas where we can have improvement.

As an example, imagine your client team having a client who did not communicate variances to a job or work spec as required. An action plan for this client may include a regular weekly email or phone call, or a communication that either you or they drive so that everybody is on the same page. Thus, removing the stress from the variance component of the contract.

When writing an action plan, it is important to think of and communicate at the level or with the knowledge that the team member has. It is pointless and somewhat soul-destroying to write an action plan for a team member who has no idea of the terminology or the expectation.

And as you are writing the action plan, it is important that the person concerned can see that their plan is part of the bigger picture. This is so as they complete their action plan, it fits like a block into the wall to get us towards the goal and to assist the team and business to get to where it wants to be.

Action plans are individual. Or at most for small groups. Because they attribute time, activity and responsibility to the individual.

So, if you have a team of 20 then you will do the action plans for the leaders, or the group leaders in the team. They will do the action plans for the people who work with them.

This individual action plan approach allows training, when you see training is needed. It allows management when you see that direction instruction or correction is needed, and it allows visibility. So you can see exactly where your team members are, or where your team leaders are.

A short and clear action plan for your clients revolves around your terms of trade. This will ensure how you and they interact and preserve a long-term profitable relationship.

An action plan for a supplier may involve the supply chain, the invoicing process, guarantees, or product performance from their point of view.

An action plan for your home team might be around the time that you need to work on the business. Support your needs in times of stress by way of quiet time or even discussion.

Again, you can create engagement by using action plans for your team around what they do, when they do it, when it's due and how you will know it is done.

Action Point 5.

Think of one of the processes that happens in your workplace with an individual, and how you might write an action plan to make this transparent and achievable for that individual.

Write down the processes that you have when you deal with a new client and turn this into an action plan.

Huddles and One-on-Ones

There is absolutely no point in having goals, action plans, or any expectations without communicating them in a clear and concise and transparent fashion with everyone involved.

I call these meetings huddles. Why? Because they should have, in my opinion, the intensity of a huddle on a sports field - when the captain, the coach, is getting the people together, finding out what's going on, what's preventing them from getting the result they want on the field, or celebrating that they're doing well but still pushing for more.

Short and sharp, is what they should be. To the point. And with an agenda.

No huddle or meeting should start without an agenda.

This is not a monthly management meeting where you might be sitting there for a period of time. This is a huddle where you're there for say 5 to 15 minutes. You're there to find out where we are, where we need to be, where we need to go, what are the holdups and how do we get over these. We're also there to celebrate where we are at, pat people on the back, and enjoy this 5 to 15 minute of positive go-forward action being led by you.

At the back of this book there is what I call a "huddle agenda ". Feel free to make up your own format, and to make it very much yours.

Every huddle starts with the "current situation". That is: *"where we are at; let's celebrate that; or what are the roadblocks to us getting on our journey and really making progress?"*

The second part of the huddle is *"what do we have to achieve in the next timeframe? What are the challenges or roadblocks to us getting there, and how can we as a team take those roadblocks apart and really go forward?"*

The last part of the huddle is: *how can you as a manager and the leader assist the team to get to do what they have to do?*

The huddle is an exercise in flowing communication. Asking the questions about where, what and how.

A Huddle with your suppliers is just that. *"Where are we at in supply of this product? The fact that it's going to be on time is good. How can we ensure that the next batch is on time as well?"* You may discuss the state of your account.

When the current situation is dealt with, then you look at the future. *"Where are we at with payments for the account? Where are we at with deliveries of product we are waiting for? How can we deal with this challenge?"*

One-on-Ones.

The one-on-one is when you look at the action plan and you speak personally/on an individual basis with the person the action plan is for. Like a huddle, it must have an agenda:

Where we at against our action plan?

What are the roadblocks to us getting to the next point we have to be according to our timeline? What resources do you need to make sure we get there?

How can I help and make this work for you?

The one-on-ones are an imperative part of making your team engaged in what they do. The more individual the one-on-one, the more engaged they will be because they're getting you; your time.

In a client One-on-One, you may be seeking feedback about work to date, about how the project is progressing. You may be seeking news or a timeline for new work.

At a supplier one-on-one you may be discussing deliveries, or availability of product.

And a home one-on-one might happen on a date night, or after a home barbecue, or at a time during the day or night when you design that this should be the one-to-one time.

In working with business owners, the most important thing I have found is a one-on-one within the home team is positioning. This not as a dumping session, but a sharing session.

I am not putting myself forward as a marriage counselor, relationship coach, or a life coach. But experience has shown me in the business community that we are better people, and our home life works better, if those around us at least have a view and understanding of the success we are having, the stress we are under, and where we are heading in the next period of time.

So, the positioning of your home team one-on-one, shall we say is imperative. And if the positioning is developed and thought through and used frequently or regularly, then everybody in the one-on-one, knows that this is a sharing session.

I'd like to share with you a couple of ideas of home team positioning that you might find useful:

1. *Hey there Susan, I just wondered if we could take 15 minutes so I could just give you some ideas about what's happening at work. Then you have some clarity around what is going on and how it*

might impact me and us in the next couple of weeks. No real big stress- just want to keep you in the loop.

2. Bob, it's been an interesting couple of weeks at work. So I wondered if I could just share with you what is going on? Just so you have an idea how I'm dealing with stuff and so you might want to give me some feedback or just listen to how things are going.

3. OK, it's time to sit down and have our little chat about what's going on at work so you know what's going on from the point of time. And so I know what's happening with the family, the sport and all of that. So why don't we do that straight after dinner when we go for a walk?

The three methods/ sentences above are just ideas to start a non-threatening involving conversation with your home team. Research shows and experience has proven that if you use similar wording on a regular basis, then the other participant in the conversation will very quickly know what to expect. They are like signals that your home team will come to recognise. This creates a sense of engagement – and a good kind of engagement.

What is imperative is that you've done a little bit of preparation and you know this is what you're going to say, and this is the information you're going to give. Interestingly enough, we all probably know exactly the reaction we're going to get from our home team.

You should cache information honestly in a really friendly fashion, and be looking for positive support and feedback.

Action Point 6

Fill out the one-on-one agendas at the back of this book for at least two of your team members.

Design and think through the positioning statement for your home team one-on-one

Celebrations and Rituals

If you've ever watched Damian McKenzie play for the All Blacks, you'll see that just before he takes a kicker goal, he stands a certain way. He looks at the goal posts, and then he smiles, and then he kicks the ball. This is his ritual before he kicks the ball. Next time you watch an All Black game, watch Damian McKenzie's kicking ritual.

There is a huge correlation between wealth, success, client stickiness, team engagement and rituals and celebration.

It is no coincidence that when we think of rituals we think of religion or sacred things.

Some of the wealthiest organisations in the world are the religious sectors - why is this?

All religions are based on a raft of rituals. The ritualistic nature of every area of religion and every area of sacred study is what holds the congregation, the membership to the religion; that is what drives their engagement.

In everything we've talked about in this chapter, the ritual of the leader's performance is important. The setting of the goals, the working through the action plans, and the one-on-ones have to be ritualistic in their intent. I'm not suggesting religious in their fervor. What I mean is there is an absolute that they will happen. It is a ritual.

The more ritualistic, the more consistent, the more driven you are as a business leader to make every step of the journey the same every time, the more successful your business will be.

This is because people engage with ritual, where they know what to expect, and it becomes a comforting thing. Rituals also guarantee that people in your teams know there is a time they will get to engage with you and raise issues and discuss things. This is a great way to ensure issues don't build up, that you know what is going on and can nip things in the bud when you need to, and that there is somewhere for all the problems to "land". Some examples of engaging rituals that you might adopt in your business are:

- Setting timelines, meeting dates, and reporting on your goals.

- Having a definitive time and an agenda for all of your one-on-one meetings.

- Celebrating when a job or work goes really well in relation to a timeline.

- The exact time of the day you call your area team members.

The agenda you run for your huddles and your action plan one-on-ones should be ritualistic.

We as human beings use rituals in our life all the time. We often don't realise that it is a ritual - we just do it because it becomes a habit or what we have always done.

How often have you heard someone say:

"This is his morning ritual."

Or have you watched a sports team and when a player is about to take a kick, or just before the start of the game, they go through their own ritual to put their head in the right space to perform that task - to perform at their best level for their game? They perform their rituals.

Rituals are the rhythms that hold a business together.

When your team starts in the morning, it could be your ritual to walk around and acknowledge every member of the team. In doing this you have a daily personal interaction with every team member.

By their feedback, by their comments, by their body language you would see how engaged they are in their activity, in their action right then right there. This might allow you to provide some direction, motivation, or inspiration to improve or train their behaviour at work.

The rituals of **celebration** are often what people remember.

The social interaction, the celebration of the time of year or a job well done, are often discussed in the workplace for many weeks or months after. This builds engagement of those people and their social interaction with your business.

The rituals of celebration are common. In the real estate industry, it's very common on the day that you take possession of your new family home for the real estate agent to deliver you a gift basket. Yes, it is a thank you, but it is also their ritual of not only thanking you but finalising the sale, looking to you for referrals and testimonials, and continuing the goodwill and the good vibe you have from buying your family home.

I worked with a building company. When their client moved into their family home, the building company would offer to put a BBQ on at their home for them. The principal leader of the building company would come and cook the barbecue and bring the wine. It was a barbecue to celebrate with the new owners of the house. It became their ritual.

In their brag book, which they used as a sales tool, were all of the photos of the different barbecues of the different houses with the different owners. Massively happy photos of people in their homes having a great time thanks to this building company.

The building company staff looked forward to it as much as the house owners. I remember well that there was one barbecue where the client did not drink. This did not stop the barbeque - it was a great barbecue with much fun. It's about the ritual; it's about the celebration.

The tighter the rituals, the more adherence you have to a ritualistic commitment, to the goals, the action plans and the outcomes, and the more successful you will be.

Action Point 7

Think of two rituals you can put in place straight away in your business.

Name one ritual celebration you can have every month with your home team.

Some simple thoughts and rules:

- *Say what you are going to do, then do it.*

- *Model what you expect to see*

- *Be gracious in defeat, humble in success.*

Chapter ten

RECRUITING FOR YOUR 4 TEAMS

With thought, planning, and process, recruitment into your four teams can provide both a better culture fit and a better end game.

The first and one of the primary rules of recruiting into your teams, has to be the fit against your values.

The values that you defined, the values that you model and the values that you and your business live, have to be aligned with, respected by, and part of any new person in the team.

Failure to align with the values of the business or yourself will lead initially to more difficult communication. That could very possibly end up in a relationship that becomes untenable.

While your core values may have slightly different definitions in each of the four teams, the values have the same behaviours and the same importance to you and your business success.

Honesty, pride, reliability, engagement, ownership are a few of the more commonly found business values. If these values are not agreed with, understood, and are provable with any new member of your team, musician in your band, or player on the field then there will be strife in the future.

Your business team

At the initial interview for anyone joining your business team, you should ask them their view on your primary values and how those values sit for them in their life? If your primary values are reliability, ownership, pride, and integrity, ask those questions specifically. Ask the person to rate out of 10 how important they are to them.

Frame the question so the person knows why they have been asked it:

We have three primary values in our company. I would like to ask you how important they are to you, and what mark out of 10 you would give them as important in your life.

Our first primary value is reliability. How important is that to you, and out of 10 what would you mark that out of 10 as important to you?

When working with business owners we have created the little worksheet as below. There is a square to mark in the number out of 10, and a little square to mark in the person's comments:

What is important to us

Reliability

Pride

Honesty

After the interview, this worksheet is attached to their employee file. As the relationship unfolds, if necessary, you can refer to this information and remind the team member that this is what they said and agreed. Much like qualifications or experience they claim.

The most important thing about this process is that you are setting up with the new team member exactly what your expectations are about these behaviours - about the values you expect, and the consistent performance of what you're doing.

Here's an example. If a person is late to work, it is not the fact that they are late to work that is the ongoing challenge. It is the ramifications of them being late to work. Extra workload or pressure on other staff members, inability to meet deadlines, processes and manufacturing that must wait for the staff, lack of efficiency etc.

The actual issue here is that the person is being unreliable; the person is not meeting one of your core values. That as a team member, or business owner you cannot rely on them to be there on time, therefore you cannot plan.

So if they are in breach of one of your primary values, then your expectation of behaviour around values has to be pointed out to them at the interview. The best way to drive this home is to get the agreement at the initial interview.

Explanation of Rules of the Game

The second thing to be done at the initial interview is to explain Rules of the Game and how they work within your environment.

A lot of our clients have Rules of the Game as a graphic. A graphic that goes on the wall in the factory, in the office, in the staff room. You can use this graphic at your interview to explain how the Rules of the Game work, and how they impact your work environment.

There should be discussion about how these rules have been agreed by all the team, and that this is how you manage, run and review the company now.

Lastly, there should be discussion about consequences for breaches, when Rules of the Game are broken.

What you're doing with both of these explanations and sets of questions is actually looking deeper into the person's work habits than what the CV says, or what they will tell you. And you're explaining at the initial interview that these are the things that you and the business and your other team members expect.

The direct result of this is that during the first period of time, or at the induction, you or the person's manager can refer to these values, behaviours and rules by way of example. You can refer to them in training by way, in any corrective language, and make sure that everybody is always on the same page.

What you model, how the team behaves, the information you give, and the rules you put in place will define the success of this team member in your environment.

Recruiting suppliers

As a business owner you have the opportunity, the responsibility and the choice to recruit suppliers for your business to work with.

Some of the usual decisions to recruit suppliers are made around brand, quality of offering, service, availability, location or price.

But bluntly speaking, you would not deal with a supplier that did not meet your primary values. It is unlikely you would deal with a supplier that was known to be dishonest. It is unlikely you would deal with a supplier that had a doubtful reputation for reliability that you could not rely on them to supply.

A good supplier by definition will meet your value statements, and abide by your Rules of the Game, because they want to deal with you. They want a quality relationship.

It is strong and meaningful to meet with the supplier and explain to them your core values, how these impact your behaviour, and your Rules of the Game.

Then, the big question has to be asked to the supplier quite definitely and quite distinctly:

"How do these values, behaviours and Rules of the Game sit with and resonate with you?"

Simply the discussion will elevate the relationship to a much deeper understanding of how the businesses will work together.

If you get a supplier that has no opinion of the values and success behaviours, then you need to consider the supplier as a risk.

Any supplier or team member that does not share your values, agree with your behaviours and want the same outcomes as you want, will sooner or later be a challenge with regards to the relationship and the performance.

Recruiting clients

Other than marketing and advertising, which are covered in many other books, recruiting clients is about recruiting people and businesses who wish to deal with your business.

Dishonesty within a client framework is a failure to communicate with regards to payment for the account, not informing you of variances to the work required, etc.

If your values are displayed on your marketing materials, on your website, in your office, and on your invoices, and your Rules of the Game are displayed and you live them, then clients will see these and know that this is how you think, feel and behave.

Every business we've ever worked with has had clients that come to the end of the road. And usually, they come to the end of the road because they're not meeting the value train, or the behaviour set that we as a business have agreed.

A lot of your values, behaviours, and expectations should be set out in your terms of trade. But if the client is going to be an ongoing client and there is an opportunity to grow that client within your business, then spend the time educating them about your values and how you see the business running. This sets out how the relationship will unfold and will definitely benefit the relationship.

This will also cause you to get feedback from the client. If you claim that reliability and performance is part of your mantra and then you don't deliver, you should fully expect the client to ring and tell you that you have told them one thing and delivered another.

What a great learning, training, and development opportunity this is for your business and your team.

Recruiting the home team

Your behaviours and your values are who you are. They will be reflected in the business and reflected at home. And recruiting your home team network to support you, is the same as you want from your other team members:

Honesty, good feedback and a transparency of outcome.

I will always remember having this discussion with a business owner, a very successful business owner about his home team:

He told me that his good lady had little idea of what went on in the office and had little interest. I asked him if when something went well in the business if they celebrated it, maybe went out for dinner or opened a nice bottle of wine? He smiled, laughed and said of "of course that's part of the benefit of being in business".

I then asked that during some of the year when times were tough, and cash was tight does he think it changed how he behaved when he was under stress?

He thought for a moment and then said "*well obviously.* "

My question was then did he think his wife noticed that when he came home on those occasions he was behaving like a bear with a sore paw.?

His answer was "*mmm probably*".

So as per normal the home team get a little bit of the benefit of when things are going well and wear the brunt of when things are not going smoothly. When things get tough and there's a knock at the door and it's a bailiff, or a creditor banging on the door, that is a very unpleasant surprise to be dealt with.

No person is an island. And I'm not suggesting that you dump, or unload all of the stuff from work into your home environment. But to have someone, your partner, a good friend maybe your brother or sister who you involve just that inch, just so they can listen to what you have to say when things are going really well and celebrate with you. Also, that they can listen and be that whiteboard when you have that question about what might be going on that may be challenging.

And it is so much more fun and pleasurable with people around you sharing the anticipation of good. And nothing good comes without work.

My favorite saying about anticipation is by Angela Carter:

ANTICIPATION IS
THE GREATER PART
OF PLEASURE

And by involving the people around you in the growth, excitement, and stuff that's happening in your business, you give them anticipation of success. But everyone is a realist, and provided you communicate and are real about what you're doing and live your values, then they will be right on the bus with you.

Chapter eleven

EPILOGUE

A few thoughts to close.

At times, being in business can be a challenge. When all is said and done, everything that comes down the pipe and comes at the business owner - you are the person making the decisions, taking the responsibility and driving everything forward. By surrounding yourself with four teams you can trust, that are reliable and deliver you a consistent level of support and outcomes, business is not only easier but a lot more fun.

And really, life is not a dress rehearsal. So you want to surround yourself with people who are sharing your journey. People who are really part of what you want to do in life and with your business.

Honesty, integrity, values. If you communicate with your four teams this way, and select your four teams to match your values and match your energy levels, then simply your business will have four rocket boosters attached to it.

Be aware that this is a process. Like recruiting your teams, as you change how you deal with your four teams, your suppliers, your clients and the people around you, people will either come on board or they will fall off. As we all know there is a natural attrition with every action we take, and everything we do - you should not be afraid of this. As you drive forward, you will find other people who are more aligned with you, and they will become part of your success journey.

Pick one of the four teams to start with. Treat the whole exercise like a Helix of four parts. And as you wind through one team increasing the involvement, the communication and the activity, the other teams will follow.

Enjoy the journey. Have some fun, laugh a lot and really enjoy your business. I look forward to hearing from you in the future, about how your four teams are going!

www.acbe.co.nz

Kerry's speaking subjects for the upcoming year:

- What I learned about businesses through Lockdown
- The Four Teams that Make and Break your Business and You
- Smart recruitment for future success
- How you write marketing scripts for your employees that really work

Tools for you to use

The Accelerators for your 4 Teams

Values

Define, Model and Live your Values - in life and in your business

Reliability	Consistency	Engagement
Accelerated By Success Behaviours	Accelerated By Rules Of the Game	Accelerated By Leadership
Definition	Definition of Rules	Desire
Alignment	Agreement from all	Honesty
Will	Constant outcomes	Knowledge
Pride	Review	Common Goals
Feedback	Visibility	Action Plans 100%
	Consequences	Huddles/One on Ones
	Recognition	Celebration/Rituals
Success behaviours are the key accelerators of RELIABILITY because they become the expected and accepted actions and reactions of all	Rules of the Game are the accelerators of CONSISTENCY because they give us the building blocks of our performance, learning and delivery	Leadership is the accelerator of Engagement because we all follow with our hearts and minds.

(Accelerators)

One on One Agenda

Date

Health and Safety. Happenings and thoughts.

What went well this week for you?

What were the challenges this week for you?

This week how can I help you?

Parked

To be got back to

Interview template

WHAT IS IMPORTANT TO US?

Reliability

Out of 10

Comments

Consistency

Comments

Pride

Comments

Honesty

Comments

Huddle Agenda

Date_____

Health and Safety.

Where did we expect to be at *right now* against our plan? (1 Min)

Where are we exactly at against our plan? (3 Min)

Reasons to celebrate, people to praise. (3 Min)

Challenges we have faced. (3 Min).

Where will we be next time we meet?

How can I help you achieve the outcome we've agreed?

Parked for future discussion:

Comments:

An Idea for an ACTION PLAN Template

ACTION PLAN						
Name						
12 Month Goal						
3 Month Goal						
Time frame						
Action Description	**Outcome**	Start date	End date	Resources Required	Learning required	Measure KPI
Potential Challenges.						
Park it.						
Opportunity						

Team Drive Quotient Metric Table

NOW

	Acknowledge	Communicate	Involve	Lead	Engage	Total
Staff						/50
Clients						/50
Suppliers						/50
Home						/50
Team drive						/200

DESIRED in 6 Months

	Acknowledge	Communicate	Involve	Lead	Engage	Total
Staff						/50
Clients						/50
Suppliers						/50
Home						/50
Team drive						/200

DESIRED in 12 Months

	Acknowledge	Communicate	Involve	Lead	Engage	Total
Staff						/50
Clients						/50
Suppliers						/50
Home						/50
Team drive						/200

Bibliography

Here is a list of some of the books I have read recently, that I have found helped with my own learning and my business journey.

This is by no means a full or exhaustive list but just a few that I heartily recommend.

Good to great	Jim Collins
The one page marketing plan	Allan Dib
Optimism	Victor Perton
Mastering the Rockefeller Habits	Vern Harnish
The E Myth	Michael Gerber
The Wealth Coach	Bradley J Sugars
The truth about employee engagement	Patrick Lencioni

Legacy	James Kerr
What you do is who you are	Ben Horowitz
The Barcelona way	Prof Damian Hughes